MW00478738

WHERE HAS THE BODY BEEN FOR 2000 YEARS?

WHERE HAS THE BODY BEEN FOR 2000 YEARS?

Church history for beginners

David Pawson

Anchor Recordings

Copyright © 2012, 2013 David Pawson

The right of David Pawson to be identified as author of this work
has been asserted by him in accordance with the
Copyright, Designs and Patents Act 1988.

First published in 2012 under the title
Where has the Church been for 2000 years?
This edition published in 2013

Published in Great Britain by Anchor Recordings Ltd.
72 The Street, Kennington, Ashford TN24 9HS UK

All rights reserved.
No part of this publication may be reproduced or transmitted
in any form or by any means, electronic or mechanical,
including photocopy, recording or any information storage
and retrieval system, without prior permission
in writing from the publisher.

www.davidpawson.org

ISBN 978-0-9569376-7-4

Contents

PREFACE

This book began as a series of informal weeknight talks given when I was pastor of two Baptist churches, one in Chalfont St Peter, Buckinghamshire, and the other in Guildford, Surrey. This explains some features.

First, the chatty style is due to the transcribing of the recordings.

Second, the reference to local geographical and historical events.

Third, I have not covered the last fifty years, which are familiar to us.

I had realised that many church members know little or nothing about the story of Christianity between the New Testament period and today. They therefore did not realise how much they have been influenced by traditions developed during that time. These can have both a negative and positive benefit.

Negative, because 'those who forget history are condemned to relive it'. Most of the mistakes we make and errors we fall into have happened before and we can learn from our forefathers to avoid them. Positive, because we have such a rich heritage it would be folly to ignore. We can draw inspiration and examples from the spiritual giants who went before us and, after all, we can look forward to meeting them personally in glory.

One welcome part of our time together was to conclude each 'lecture' by singing hymns written in the period we had reviewed, which brought us in direct contact with their love for our Lord. Those whose worship is largely made up of contemporary choruses are losing out on the buried treasure in older hymn books.

I would not pretend that this is a complete or even adequate history of the church. Regard it as a collection of impressionistic sketches. My interest throughout was in what we can learn from the past for our own task in the present.

J. David Pawson

1
HOW DID THE EARLY CHURCH CAPTURE THE WORLD?
AD 30 – 400

Their voice has gone out to all the earth and their words to the end of the world.

ROMANS 10:18

It is the most amazing story. From the year AD 30 to the year AD 400, beginning with a handful of fishermen, Christianity spread throughout the then known world, until it replaced many other religions. They did it without an army (but they fought well), without money, without influential people, and they did it with all the might and power of the Roman Empire against them. I want to try and analyse for you how they accomplished such a victory.

In the Acts of the Apostles, we have the first thirty years of church history, from about AD 30–60. Yet it is an unfinished story. Acts has been described in these terms: how they brought the good news from Jerusalem to Rome – from the capital of the sacred world to the capital of the secular world. But it went on spreading out in ripples.

We can summarise the situation by the time the

story of the New Testament church closes. The new believers were greatly helped by these things:

- Straight Roman roads provided access around the Mediterranean world.
- A common language was spoken – Greek.
- There was peace – the famous *pax Romana*.
- They could travel from one country to another without travel documents.
- In most large towns and even some smaller ones, there were groups of Jews who already knew the Old Testament scriptures and were ready to listen.
- The whole empire was morally and spiritually sick.

Nevertheless, it was still an astonishing triumph! The people who spread the church included official missionaries (*apostles*, as the New Testament calls them) but were mainly ordinary men and women. Commercial travellers of the ancient world first established churches. It looks as if no-one knows who established the church of Rome. Paul didn't, and in spite of what some say, Peter didn't either. It looks as if a group of ordinary travellers who had to go to Rome started the church there.

The church was not made up of the influential (see 1 Corinthians 1:26-31), and it included slaves, of whom there were sixty million in the Roman Empire. How did those early believers win the Roman Empire, without buildings, denominational headquarters, financial resources or committees? Their organisation was utterly simple. They just had local groups of Christians which they called *churches*, and each church had elders to lead them spiritually and deacons to serve them practically. Between the churches moved the apostles, who planted new churches and acted as pioneers, and evangelists who came to preach the gospel and get folk converted, and prophets, who came to speak the word of God to people. That is the only organisation you can find in the New Testament.

Their worship was utterly simple. They baptised believers by immersion in water. They had bread and wine at the Lord's Supper and their worship was a mixture of fixed prayers and free prayer. That comes out clearly in the New Testament. People in the congregation prayed. They also said prayers together which were of fixed form. They were fond of singing, though they had no musical instrument and no choirs. They sang psalms from the Old Testament, hymns of the Christians and spiritual songs (which is a special form of singing in the Spirit known only to Christians). This was their life!

They spread from place to place. We will take up the story at the end of Acts, in the year AD 60, and I want to describe how from that position, with a tiny group of Christians in every major city around the eastern shores of the Mediterranean, they spread from being a minority movement to the point where it could be said that the pagan temples were deserted, and where the Roman Empire and even the Emperor himself was in church on Sunday, worshipping Jesus Christ!

How did they do it? They did it by realising that there were three major battles that Christians had to fight, and in the first four centuries they fought these battles, in each one gaining the victory: a spiritual battle that began with the Jews; a mental battle that began with the Greeks; a physical battle that began with the Romans. Today, *we* are engaged in these three battles. You can learn from history how to fight them, and what it costs to be a soldier of the Lord Jesus Christ.

A SPIRITUAL BATTLE –
WITH OTHER RELIGIONS

There is a popular idea abroad today, and it was around then, that Christianity must be mixed with other religions – that all religions are basically the same, that we are all travelling to the same God, that we will all finish up in the same place and that Christianity is only one religion among others and can be compared and contrasted with all the others. I once picked up a young student hitch-hiker. I asked, 'What are you training to do?'

'To become a teacher.'

'What will you teach?'

'Religious Knowledge.'

'Oh, so you believe in God?'

'No, I don't.'

'Then why teach Religious Knowledge?'

'I am going to teach children in the school I go to all the religions of the world and I'm going to show them that basically they are all the same.'

Now this was the spiritual battle they had to fight in the first four centuries. They had to fight for the understanding that Christianity is unique and that you can't put it among the religions. You can't mix it with any other. It would have been absolutely fatal if they had done so. If the Christians had given way at this point in the first four centuries, we would not be in church on Sundays, and it is doubtful if we would ever have heard of Jesus Christ. This was the spiritual battle, and it began with the Jews.

You have a tinge of this in the New Testament already. Here you have the Jews saying to the Christians, 'You must mix your religion with ours.' The very first man to give his life for Jesus Christ was a man who said, 'We'll never mix Christianity with Judaism. Judaism is obsolete.' The man's name was Stephen, and as he argued most skilfully and lovingly and firmly that Christianity won't mix with that religion of the Jews, they were so angry that they took him outside the city wall and threw rocks at him until he died. Stephen was the first martyr. He died for this one thing: Christianity will not mix with any other religion. It is unique. It is unique because it is exclusive. It is exclusive because Jesus is the only Son of God and because Jesus made it exclusive and said, 'There is only *one*

way you will ever get to the Father and it's by me!'
Therefore in no other name under heaven is there
salvation, except in the name of Jesus.

Now it is interesting that Jesus himself knew that
Christian religion would not mix with the Jewish.
He said it is like putting new wine in old bottles to
do that. It is like taking a piece of new cloth that
has never been shrunk and sewing it onto a hole
or patch. Sooner or later you will find it will pull
away. You cannot mix the two. That battle was
fought very fiercely. Paul fought it. Peter was flung
into the battle against his wish. God had to teach
him a lesson; and others fought it, as we see in the
letter to the Hebrews.

Finally, in AD70, the Temple in Jerusalem
crashed. It was ruined by the Roman soldiers. You
might have thought that would have been the end of
Judaism – but it was not. Later still, you find such
strange sects as the Nazarenes and the Ebionites
– people who tried to put Christians under the
Jewish law. They did it for three hundred years. The
people who are doing it today are the Seventh-day
Adventists – many of whom are good Christians,
but they are trying to bring us back under the
Sabbath law of the seventh day. It is a battle that
we are still having to fight. This is very up-to-date.
Finally, it was established that you could become a
Christian without becoming a Jew – and the battle
was won! Christianity was unique.

After winning that side of the battle, they were
straight into another side. What about all the other

religions? If you want to study religions, study the Roman Empire. You name it, they had it. You could shop around in the religions' supermarket in Rome and you could buy almost any idol you wished. You could choose your religion just like that.

I remember going to the Pantheon – one of the most amazing buildings I have ever been in. Its name means *the house of all gods*. There it is in Rome, built in BC 27, still standing after 2000 years. It is built like the Royal Albert Hall, albeit a bit smaller with a hole in the middle of the roof and a great dome ceiling. Unlike the R.A.H. it has nothing in it except, round the edge, it has niches in which were all the gods of the Roman Empire. As soon as a new religion came into the empire, into a niche went their god. This was their policy – a policy we call *syncretism* which means, *mix your religion*. Since the Roman Empire kept getting bigger, bringing in new people with new cultures and new religions, all they did was add gods to the Pantheon.

There was one niche which they offered to the Christians for a statue of Jesus Christ. The Christians said, 'Never!' Jesus never went into that Pantheon. But when I went into it, all the niches were empty, except there was a statue of Jesus in one of them. It had been taken over by the church, and is now a place of worship. It is interesting. Jesus Christ would not be thought of as he is today (in the world's thinking) if he had been put in one of those niches with the others.

This was the battle they had to fight. They had said, 'We will not mix our religion with the others.' This caused real trouble, because the Romans registered all religions. When you were registered you became a *Religio licita*. You were not an illicit faith any more, you were a 'licita' faith, a legal faith, and this was added to the list. Now the Christians refused to become a *Religio licita*. You might have said, 'That was silly. This was sticking their necks out.' But they said, 'We're not going to have Christianity in that list of religions. We are not a religion. We are followers of Jesus Christ.' Gradually the other religions became established in Rome, and finally they put a statue of Caesar in a niche. The day came when Caesar was regarded as god. The Roman Empire said: our religion is the worship of Caesar; from now on you pray to Caesar; from now on you burn incense to Caesar; from now on you say, 'Caesar is lord'. That is when the physical battle began for the Christians. More of that later.

But the interesting thing is that the charge of atheism went both ways. The Romans accused the Christians of being atheists, and the Christians accused the Romans of being atheists. On what grounds did they say this? Well, the Romans said, 'You Christians are atheists because you don't believe in the gods of Rome.' And they didn't. They said, 'The idols are nothing. The gods don't exist.' And the Christians said to the Romans, 'You are atheists.' The word *atheist* occurs once in the

Bible – Ephesians chapter 2, where Paul said, 'You were Gentiles, you were pagans, you were without God and without hope in the world.' And the word translated *without God* is *atheas* – and an atheist is not someone who does not *believe* in God, but someone who is *without* God. An atheist may go to a temple, he may bow down to an idol, but he is without God. That is the real meaning of the word *atheist*. There are millions of atheists. They are not irreligious. They say their prayers. If you pressed them they would say they believe in something, somewhere, or someone up there. But they are atheists – they do not know God; they do not have his grace and his power and his salvation in their lives.

So the Romans said to the Christians, 'You are atheists; you don't believe in the gods', and the Christians said, 'You are atheists; with all your gods, you don't have God.' That is why Paul said at Athens, 'I have seen all your altars', but, he said, 'I noticed one at the end, "To the god we don't know"'. Well, I've come to talk to you about that God, the One you don't know.' (See Acts 17:23.)

That was the spiritual battle, and we are still fighting it today. In a so-called Christian church – the most prominent church in Cambridge – there was held a service for the World Congress of Faiths. Into that Congress came Buddhists, Hindus, Bahais, Jews, Christians, the lot. They met to worship together, and they were there to pretend that all religion is one. They met under a man who had been ordained to preach the Christian gospel. That is the battle we have to fight. If that is happening, believe me, this is going to be *the* battle of the future. For there is a growing move towards what the Bible always predicted would happen in history – towards *one world religion*. At that point the Christians say no. Our religion is unique. It will not mix with any other. One of the conditions of joining in that service was that Christ should not be mentioned. That gives the whole game away at once. This is a battle we shall have to fight ever more fiercely. We refuse to put Jesus Christ alongside Buddha, or Mohammed, or anyone else. He is the *only* Son of God. And we refuse to put Christianity in a basin with all the other religions and mix it up and call it *faith*. We *refuse* to do this.

But the Bible also predicts that those who refuse to do it will come to a time when they will not even be allowed to shop for food, until they accept this one world religion. Persecution will come this way. It is a battle we may have to fight in our lifetime. It is already on our shores and in our churches, and it is a battle that in the first four hundred years they fought and won. We would not have Christianity today if they had not fought it. Do you see why I am writing about the past? Because it is not just the past – it is the present too.

A MENTAL BATTLE THAT BEGAN
WITH THE GREEKS

The next battle was not with religion but with philosophy, and it was a battle not with the Jews, but with the Greeks. The Greeks were the brilliant thinkers, the intellectuals, the know-alls. The Greeks were the scholars, the students, the philosophers. Sooner or later, Christianity was going to come into contact with the intellectuals. The biggest danger then was going to be that the intellectuals would succeed in altering Christianity, in producing what they said would be a more superior form of it, in compromising and changing the truth to fit the intellect. This is still one of the major battles we have to fight. Christianity cannot be altered to fit the intellect. There are many questions that I have with my intellect that I have still not answered. But, thank God, I got to the point where I was prepared to *believe* before I got my intellect entirely satisfied.

Let us see what happened. This was a much more difficult battle because it was a battle inside the church, not outside it. It was a battle that had to be fought with words and with the pen. Some of the best writings we have from the history of the early church come from this battle.

A man called Irenaeus wrote five books under the title *Against Heresies*. We can thank God he did. He was one of the great soldiers of this battle. Another man called Origen wrote 6,000 books, letters and pamphlets in this battle. Think of the labours of that man. I have got a little book which contains most of those writings which are the words that were *weapons* in this battle. We will look at some of the things they had to fight.

There was a man called Marcion. You would think this was some youngster today in the senior class of a school talking. Marcion said: I don't like a God of wrath, and I can't understand the God of the Old Testament, and I am quite sure the God of the Old Testament is a different God from the God of the New Testament and Jesus. I have had that said to me by young people today. So he went on to say: we will cut the Old Testament out of the Bible; we are going to be New Testament people. So he cut that out. Then he found to his dismay that he had to start chopping some of the New Testament out. He did not like the book of Revelation at all. That was too much like the Old Testament. So that went out. With his scissors in his hand he began to look at Paul, and he said, 'You know, Paul said some rather nasty things.' Out they went. Then he found that even in the Gospels there were passages that he was not altogether happy about. Jesus said a few things that he should not have said. He was the first to discover that when you apply scissors to the Bible you cannot stop.

Here was one of the first battles. And he finished up with two gods – the God of the Old Testament and the God of the New. That is a heresy we still have to fight. So people fought it, and the reason why we are able to read from both the Old and the

New Testaments and read the whole Word of God today, is because Marcion lost that battle – because the Christians said, 'We are going to stay with the whole Word. However difficult it is to understand things in the Old Testament, or even in the New, for that matter, however difficult my intellect finds it, we are not going to start cutting about this Book until we understand it.' The battle was won, and we have the whole Bible today.

Another much bigger difficulty was with *Gnosticism*. A gnostic is the opposite of an agnostic. An agnostic is someone who doesn't know. A gnostic is someone who does. And there were a lot of Greeks who said, 'I am a gnostic. I know!' There were a lot of intellectual know-alls around, and they criticised Christianity. What was the basic fault with this thinking? It was a mixture of thought. It came partly from Egypt, partly from Persia, and some of it seems to have come from India. But the basic philosophy was this: spiritual things are good, material things are bad. Many people think this way. Even people called Christians can think this way and fall into this kind of trap. Now see where this led them. They then said, 'Well now, if matter is bad, God couldn't have created it.' That led them to deny a fundamental truth. Then they said, 'If matter is evil, Jesus could never have taken a body of flesh.' So they began to teach that Jesus only appeared to be a body, that he was really a phantom all the time, that he wasn't real and that he was never hungry or tired. Then they went further, and said, 'Jesus couldn't have died because matter is evil and Jesus couldn't have been matter, and it is only material beings that die.' Then they went further still and they said, 'The idea of a resurrection of the body is ridiculous.'

So they went on. Having started with this basic wrong idea that matter is evil and spirit is good, everything else went wrong – as today it goes wrong in Christian Science, which is one of the modern forms of this kind of thinking. We are still fighting the same old battle.

So the greatest minds of the church set themselves to deal with this problem. If you want to know why John wrote his Gospel and why John wrote his first letter, the answer is that he was fighting this thinking in the church. He was saying, 'Listen. The Word was God, and the Word was made flesh. Do you get that?' And he said, 'That which we have handled and seen, we declare to you – Jesus!' He was fighting this already, and it took them about 150 years to fight it. Gnostics were saying that Jesus, the Son of God, was never truly man. But if you deny that he was truly man, you deny the faith. You have cut away the very heart of our faith that Jesus was able to help us because he took flesh like us, that he knows what our temptations are, because he had a body like mine, that he really did become man. This was a denial of that.

We will mention briefly the names of some of the greatest minds. Tertullian, in a town called Carthage in North Africa, wrote against Gnosticism, as did

Clement and Origen (living in Alexandria) and Cyprian. Since we have most of their writings even today, we can read how they fought with their pen and with their voices against what they knew could destroy the Christian faith.

Another battle was not just with what people said about Christ, but with what people said about Christians. They were slandered. Some would say, 'They are cannibals – we hear that they eat bodies and drink blood.' Some said, 'It's dreadful – the sexual orgies that go on in that church, "Love Feasts" they call them.' They even said that Christians got an ass's head and stuck it on a pole and worshipped it. Some of the writings we have are from people who defended Christians against such slanders. They were fighting a mental battle. Three things they did in fighting this battle make us grateful to them.

The first thing was this. How were they to say quite definitely what was the true faith when so many Christian preachers were declaring this new kind of thinking – this 'philosophical' kind of gospel? The answer is that they decided to put together all the books that went back to the apostles and to call it the scripture. By AD 200 they had put together all the books that went back directly to the apostles who got the truth first-hand from Jesus. That is how the New Testament was put together: the canon of scripture was the result of this battle. (Many other people were writing false gospels about Jesus, false epistles of Paul and false books claiming that they were the truth. Even Paul, in his letter to the Thessalonians, said, 'Don't be bothered by any letter that purports to come from me. Every letter from me will be signed in my hand.')

The second thing they did was to state the faith in what were called *creeds* (from the word *credo*, I believe). They used to make lists of what they believed, as opposed to these gnostics. Here is the beginning of one: 'I believe in God the Father Almighty, Maker of heaven and earth'. The gnostics said, 'Matter is evil so God didn't make matter.' The Christians said, 'I believe in God the Father Almighty, Maker of heaven and earth, and in Jesus Christ, His only Son, who was conceived by the Holy Ghost, born of the Virgin Mary . . . .' He was no phantom. He was conceived. He was born. And then they said, 'Suffered under Pontius Pilate, crucified, dead and buried'. He did die! He had a real body on that cross! And all the way through – 'I believe in the resurrection of the body, and the life everlasting'. They were fighting this battle, and they said, 'This is what we believe.' And we can still recite the creeds and say, 'This is what we believe too!'

The third thing they did was to get together in councils, not to organise the church but to share with each other the battle, close their ranks, and fight for the faith. Today Christians still do this.

This battle is being fought *today*. One philosophy we must fight today is not called Gnosticism, but *existentialism*. Even if you have never heard that word you are meeting it almost every day. You will find it in the literature of Jean-Paul Sartre. You will find it in the music of Debussy. You will find it in the art of Picasso. You will find it in the culture of our day. You will find it in the drug taking culture. You will find it in Marshall McLuhan's often quoted statement that the medium is the message. In theology you can find it in the writings of Bultmann, Tillich and many others. Their names may mean nothing to you, but the names of two men who popularised that kind of thinking in the twentieth century may be more familiar to some: John Robinson, who was Bishop of Woolwich, and Howard Williams, sometime President of the Baptist Union. They were amongst those (and there have been many others since then) who have re-defined Christianity in the terms of a pagan philosophy that is basically atheist and presents God as being impersonal and even non-existent.

Have you heard the phrase 'God is dead'? That is the result of Christian theologians following this philosophy. The mental battle still needs the finest brains we can produce. It must be fought with words and pens, and we must have the courage to say this is *not* the Christian faith.

We should refuse to have anyone preaching in our churches who makes such 'existentialist' statements. It is a battle. We may not have to fight the physical battles that so many others have had to fight, and maybe you have thought, 'Why is it so easy here?' But it is *not* easy here; there is another kind of battle and it is, from one point of view, much more subtle, and therefore more difficult. The physical battle is straightforward. You know where you are. You know that you are going to suffer. You know which side you are on. They deny what you stand for. You affirm it. That is the straightforward battle, hard though it is. But the battle that we will need to fight is this mental battle. The early church fought it and won. It is interesting that one of the issues over which they fought has popped up again with the Jehovah's Witnesses. And it is about 1,700 years old, though they do not realise that. We are fighting it.

Coming in the name of Christ – that is the problem. If a man comes in the name of the devil, you know where you are. But when he comes in the name of Jesus Christ, and says, 'This is the new theology, the new morality, the new gospel, the new Christianity', you need to say, 'There is no *new* Christianity, there is only the *old* one' – and we are to contend for the faith once delivered to the saints. In the first four hundred years they fought this battle inside the church and they won. That is why we have the church today.

A PHYSICAL BATTLE THAT BEGAN
WITH THE ROMANS

The church never used physical force to establish the gospel in the first four centuries (the Inquisition was to come later). They used love to win people for the Lord, but physical force was used against them again and again.

Why did the Christians suffer so much? People have said it was because of those rumours and slanders (about 'cannibalism' and 'orgies'). People have said it was because they would not join in the social customs of idolatry and the games and the circuses of Rome. People said it was because they were so intolerant of other religions. People have said it is because they were a secret society and were a threat to the internal security of the empire. I want to say it was none of those things.

The reason so many believers have suffered so much is there in the words of Jesus, 'They have hated me without a cause.' So here is the only possible explanation for the sufferings of Christians – there isn't one. The people, in the depths of their hearts, so hate God that they hate his people without a reason. There is an irrational dislike of Christians in the world. There is something you can't explain about this anti-Christianism. And the other side of anti-Semitism is the attitude of the Jews to the Christians. It was the Jews who first caused the sufferings of Christians, again and again. There is no reason for it. But let me tell you about it. I don't want to play on your emotions, but I want to tell you of some of the martyrs, some of the sufferers.

It began in the days of Nero in AD 64. One day, some years ago, I stood in the ruins of the gardens of the palace of Nero. They are beautiful gardens with flowers, but I knew that the soil was drenched with blood. The mad Emperor Nero, in his ambition to rebuild Rome as a metropolis, had the city set on fire – so history supposes – and 14 out of 17 districts were razed to the ground and hundreds were burnt to death. Nero is said to have played a fiddle while Rome burnt. But when he began to be blamed for it, he looked round for a scapegoat and said, 'The Christians did it and we'll arrest and punish them.' Punish them he did. He arrested every Christian within reach of Rome. He tore the skins off wild beasts and he clothed them in those skins and set his dogs on them. He beheaded them. He crucified them. Finally, to satiate his malice, he covered them with pitch and stuck them in barrels while they were still alive, and then lit them to be torches for his garden, while he drove madly round in a chariot. That was Nero.

That sparked off the sufferings of the Christian. And between then and AD 300 they suffered ten periods of the most frightful persecution that the church has ever known. I have a little book known as *Foxe's Book of Martyrs* which I picked up on a barrow somewhere. It used to be compulsory Sunday reading for Christians. You ought to read it some time. It shows until the date it was written that there had not been a period of ten years without

Christians suffering martyrdom, and there still hasn't. Read the early chapters about the early persecutions of the church.

The next great persecution was around AD 100. One of the men to suffer in that persecution was called John, the last of the twelve apostles. He was sent to the salt mines; then he was sent to the little island of Patmos, in the Aegean Sea, and was chained to the wall of his prison. Out of that prison cell came the book of Revelation. You can lock people in, but as Paul said from prison, 'I may be in chains, but the word of God is not bound.'

In AD 110 a new Governor, Pliny, took up residence in Asia Minor. When he got there he was astonished to see that the temples were deserted and the idolatrous shrines had no business. So he said, 'What has gone wrong? These are the gods of our great Roman Empire! Why does nobody come?' And they said, 'The Christians – there are too many of them.' He replied, 'Christians – that superstitious people? Arrest them.' He arrested them, and he asked people to tell him who they were. Everyone who was betrayed was arrested and put to death. But finally Pliny got so puzzled – first by the number of Christians, they just kept coming, and, secondly, by the quality of their lives. He said, 'I must find out more about these people.' One day he sent his spy into one of their early morning services. The spy came back and reported his trip to Pliny: 'They meet before daybreak. They sing hymns to Christ as God. Then they take an oath, a promise (in

Latin, a *sacramentum*) to Jesus as Lord, and they promise not to steal and not to commit adultery and not to murder.' Pliny was puzzled by this. He wrote off to the Emperor Trajan straight away. He wrote, 'Dear Trajan, I am arresting Christians, and I am putting them to death, but I'm a bit puzzled by what I find. What shall I do?' Trajan wrote back and said, 'Well, we had better go carefully. If they are betrayed, don't listen to anonymous betrayals.'

This did ease the situation in Asia Minor. But he said, 'If they are shown to you to be an anti-Roman religion, then you must test them by asking them whether they will say, "Caesar is lord", and if they won't say it, you have got to put them to death.' So many still died.

We pass on now some years to a man called Ignatius. The story about him is wonderful. He was one of the youngest ministers of the church in those days. They called them *bishops* then. Every church had its bishop. It was just the name for a minister. He was the bishop of Antioch. He was arrested by the Romans and given the test. He failed to do it, so he was escorted to the Colosseum in Rome where he was to be thrown to the wild beasts. But his escorted journey to Rome is just a pageant of triumph! Christians would leave their homes and they would walk along with him for a few miles. In fact, he hardly had to walk a mile without Christians. They came and walked with him and had fellowship and he spoke to them as he went to his death. Oh, what does a man say to his fellow Christians when he is walking to his death? He said wonderful things. But I have written down one thing he said: 'Now I begin to be a disciple. He who is near the sword is near to God. He who is among the wild beasts is in company with God.' This was a man who went to his death. He wrote letters every night when he rested, chained to his Roman soldier. He wrote one of his last letters to another minister in a place called Smyrna, a man called Polycarp. He wrote this: 'Stand fast, firm as an anvil, though often smitten.'

Forty years later, Polycarp was martyred and this is how it happened. Polycarp was a very old man by this time. One day they held the Roman games in honour of the Emperor, in the town of Smyrna, where Polycarp was the Christian bishop. The games got so exciting, the blood began to flow, and the crowd got worked up. Then somebody cried, 'Away with the atheists'. They dragged eleven Christians into the arena, called them 'atheists' and then set the lions onto them. Finally, things got so out of hand that the crowd began to cry for the blood of Polycarp. A Roman soldier was despatched with a few other soldiers to go and arrest him, and they came to a little cottage outside Smyrna where Polycarp lived. They knocked at the door and he came to answer. They did not recognise him, for they didn't know him. They asked, 'Is there a man called Polycarp here?' He could have said, 'No, he has gone out', and he said later that he was tempted to do so. But the Lord gave him the victory, and he said, 'I am Polycarp.' Then he held out his wrists for the chains, and he was led into the arena. When the Governor saw how old he was he said, 'Have pity upon your white hairs. Just curse Christ and you can go back to your cottage.' And Polycarp said this, 'Eighty and six years have I served him and he has never done me wrong. How then can I blaspheme now my King, whom I serve?' They could do nothing but kill him. The lions had been taken away so they built a bonfire and tied him to the stake. But the wind was strong, and it blew the winds away from Polycarp, which deeply impressed the crowd. Finally, a Roman soldier, out of pity for the old man, plunged a dagger into his heart. The Christians recorded that martyrdom and they finished the record with these words: 'Quintus statius Quadratus' ... 'but Jesus Christ will be King forever'. That man's name, Quadratus, goes down as the Governor, but Jesus Christ's name goes down as King!

We turn the pages of history and come to the year 177. Severe persecution now breaks out in a place called Lyons in France. The aged minister of Christ, Pothinus, was thrown into jail, and remained there until his death.

Then they took a little slave girl in her teens, a girl whose name has gone down into the annals of history. 'A noble army, matron and maid' – maybe you have sung it! This little maid, Blandina, was taken and subjected to the most incredible torture. This is what was said of her: 'The tormentors tortured her from morning until evening, until they were tired and weary and acknowledged that they were conquered and could do no more to her. Her comfort and recreation and relief from the pain of her sufferings was in exclaiming, "I am a Christian and there is nothing vile done by us!" The next day they took her into the arena. After the scourging, after the wild beasts, after the roasting seat, she was finally enclosed in a net and thrown before a bull, and having been tossed about by that animal she also was sacrificed. She, like a noble mother who had cheered on her children, hastened with them with joy and exultation as if they were bidden to a marriage feast!' So died Blandina.

Turn the pages and we come to a North African prison where a Christian woman is put in jail with her baby in the next cell. The baby is starving but she is not allowed to feed it, and no-one else does. Her breasts are swollen and sore; the baby is crying for milk. They say, 'You can feed your baby as soon as you say, "Caesar is lord".' Could you take that? This is what she said: 'We give honour to Caesar as Caesar. But we render fear and worship to Christ as Lord!' What a battle!

Under Decius, the Roman Governor, a long calm (a calm that had lasted about thirty years) broke. For the first time Rome systematically set out to crush Christianity throughout the whole empire. For the first time, it was not local but universal. And the sufferings of that time I just cannot go into any more. But after Decius there were forty years of peace, and the church grew in numbers, wealth and influence and, alas, that is what tends to happen in times of ease.

Then finally, Satan's last fling came under the Emperor Diocletian. In the year 303 he ordered every church to be destroyed, for now they had started building churches. He ordered every Bible to be burned, every Christian in a Roman official position to be sacked, and every Christian to be beheaded, burned or drowned. Satan knew he was losing the battle. There were so many Christians now, the Empire was being overrun. This was the final battle, and it was won!

There are two major things still to be said about all this persecution. Firstly, we know many of the martyrs, but we know too the very sad fact that thousands of Christians were defeated by the persecutions. Some of them gave in and said, 'Caesar is lord'. Some of them bribed the officials with money to get off. Some of them ran away to other countries. Many of them, alas, gave in. Imagine that some in your church were subject to such persecution, and suppose some of those arrested had the grace and courage to die for the Lord. Supposing also that some, when faced with the test, gave way and denied that they knew Christ and never came near us. Then suppose that later, when peace came, they wanted to come back into the church. What should we do?

That problem tore the church in two when the easier time came. Some said, 'They can't be

Christians. They let the Lord down. They denied him. They wouldn't come near us when the persecution was on. Why should they come into membership now?' I am afraid that split the church.

Secondly, the church never grew so strongly, or so quickly, as under those sufferings. It caused that Northern African Christian, Tertullian, to say: 'The blood of the martyrs is the seed of the church. If you want to plant a church, plant a martyr.' The sad thing is that the church of Christ has never grown so quickly, in proportion to its members, as it did in the first three hundred years. That is the answer to the suffering. I cannot understand it, yet it is true, that where a church suffers, it grows. Why? Because, I think, it sorts out the membership: it reduces Gideon's men to the three hundred who can take it; it really makes the church what it ought to be – a noble army!

It is time to draw these threads to a conclusion. We have gone through three centuries, and we have come to the year 312. In that year, the Roman Emperor Constantine himself became a Christian. It is the strangest story and I cannot sort out truth from fiction. But there is a certain bridge, the Milvian Bridge, on the north side of Rome. Constantine went out to meet the enemies of Rome, and he saw a vision in the sky. He saw a cross, and he heard a voice: 'In this sign, conquer.' So he painted that cross on the shield of every Roman soldier, and he said, 'From now on I am a Christian and so are you.'

I am not sure that was a good thing. But the

Emperor became a Christian. He said, 'From now on Sunday will be a day of rest.' That was the first time Sunday ever was a day of rest. The Christians had never had Sunday until then. He also said, 'Women are going to be valued more highly in the empire.' He said, 'Slaves are going to be treated properly.' The emperor was Christian, and that was the end of the physical battle – at least in the Roman Empire. It was the end of the persecutions and the sufferings. But may I say this: it was not quite the end of the other two battles and I just have a few more comments to make about those.

Constantine, to his alarm, discovered that the church was in a most dreadful state. They were arguing, quarrelling and falling out over something. He looked into this and said, 'What a church! Now that it is free it is arguing.' At first he dismissed it as bad temper and doctrinal quibbling and personalities. Then he looked into it more carefully and realised that the mental battle was still on.

Away in Alexandria was a most powerful preacher. He was tall and handsome, an orator, a singer who wrote music as well. He had a huge church and he was preaching something dreadful. He was preaching exactly what the Jehovah's Witnesses are preaching today – that Jesus is not quite God. This great orator, with his attractive personality, had scores of other people. You will remember that the first mental battle with Gnosticism was a battle against the idea that Jesus was not fully man, but now the other side of the battle was the claim that Jesus was not fully God. This man's name was Arius. His heresy swept right through the church like a craze, a fashion. Other preachers were getting up in their pulpits and saying that Jesus was not fully God; that he was created, not begotten; that he was only the Son of God, not God. They began to destroy the faith that way.

There was one man who could see what was happening, and only one at first. His name was Athanasius. He was a young man, a deacon, whereas Arius was a bishop. And this young fair-haired man was very small. People said that he was a dwarf because he was so tiny. This tiny, fair-haired deacon of a church said, 'That is not the Christian truth, and I will fight it.' It led to a proverb, 'Athanasius is against the world' (*Athanasius contra mundum*) because the world had gone after Arius. But Athanasius said, 'I will fight it. This is something I've got to quarrel about. This is something I've got to fight.' Jesus was fully God as well as fully man. And however attractive and popular the preacher, if he says Jesus is not fully God, he destroys the faith. How can Jesus bring God and man together unless he is fully God and fully man? That is the simple truth, and Athanasius saw it.

So finally Constantine said, 'Look, we will have to settle this once and for all', and he called around three hundred bishops together. He hadn't a room big enough in his palace. By the way, he had moved from Rome and decided to set up house in Byzantium, renaming it Constantinople. As he could not find a room big enough, they went over the Sea of Bosphorus (or the Sea of Marmara, as it was called) to a town called Nicaea. And there in a large church, those bishops met. They bore on their own bodies the marks of their sufferings; the maimed and the lame came in, and the Roman Emperor greeted them. What a dramatic moment!

The physical battle was certainly over, but the battle went on. In a room outside the church was Athanasius. He was too young to be allowed into the main discussion, but he was the main figure in it. He fed all his arguments through a friend into the main discussion. And the friend kept running out, and saying to Athanasius, 'They said this, what do you say now?' And he said, 'Tell them this scripture.' Back in went the man, who told them the text and said, 'This is the word of God.' Athanasius fought the battle from outside the Council!

They split over two Greek words: *homoousios* and *homoiousios*. People thought: fancy splitting the church over a word! But it was an important word. *Homoousios* (pronounced *homo-ousios*) means 'of one and the same substance'. *Homoiousios* (pronounced *homoy-ousios*) means 'of like substance'. The split was over this issue: is Jesus of the *same substance* as God, or is he just *like* God? While Athanasius fought it from outside, Arius, that commanding preacher, beguiled them inside the assembly, but thank God the battle was won by Athanasius.

God chooses nobodies. Five times Athanasius had to run for his life, and he was in exile, but he continued to fight because the council of Nicaea did not settle it. What they did do was to produce a statement (in 325; with additions made at the Council of Constantinople, 381) which is still used in worship. It is called the 'Nicene Creed'. Here is a translation of its earliest (325) version:

We believe in one God, the Father Almighty, Maker of all things visible and invisible. And in one Lord Jesus Christ, the Son of God, begotten of the Father the only-begotten; that is, of the essence of the Father, God of God, Light of Light, very God of very God, begotten, not made, being of one substance with the Father; By whom all things were made both in heaven and on earth; Who for us men, and for our salvation, came down and was incarnate and was made man; He suffered, and the third day he rose again, ascended into heaven; From thence he shall come to judge the quick and the dead. And in the Holy Ghost. But those who say: 'There was a time when he was not;' and 'He was not before he was made;' and 'He was made out of nothing,' or 'He is of another substance' or 'essence,' or 'The Son of God is created,' or 'changeable,' or 'alterable' — they are condemned by the holy catholic and apostolic church.

Ever since then the church of Jesus Christ has declared in its creeds the truth that Jesus is fully God – 'very God of very God'. Every Christmas we sing it: 'Hark, the herald angels sing', 'True God of True God', 'Light of Light', 'Lo, he abhors not the Virgin's womb'. 'Begotten, not created'. We are singing what was settled at Nicea. Jesus is fully God.

THE MENTAL BATTLE WAS WON BY AD 400

The spiritual battle continued. Constantine had two grandsons, one called Julian, and they said, 'We don't like what our grandfather did.' This is not unusual. The grandsons said, 'Now we are going to turn the clock back. We are going to re-introduce the Roman pagan gods, and the temples, and open them up again,' and they did. But no-one came, and they realised it was too late! The spiritual battle had been won.

By the year 400 there was only one religion, which you saw prominent through the whole Roman Empire. Roman soldiers brought it to England. St Alban was the first martyr in Britain – a Roman soldier dying for Jesus Christ. We still call the place St Alban's. The faith had spread down into Africa. It had spread east into Syria, and into India. The then known world had heard. The physical battle was won, the mental battle was won, and the church had captured the world for Jesus Christ.

Yet we are still fighting this battle, and it is fiercer than ever before. In many countries it was and sometimes still is a *physical* battle. In Europe it was (and still is) a *mental* battle. In 1517 Martin Luther nailed to the church door what *he* believed was the truth. Where should we go and nail things today?

It is a mental battle today *inside* the church. Are we ready to face and to fight it with all that it involves? It can be painful. And the agony of *mind* is worse than the agony of *body*.

Richard Wurmbrand (1909-2001), a well-known Romanian Christian minister who was imprisoned and tortured repeatedly for his faith in Jesus Christ during the communist era, said that he suffered more in the West than in his native country, and he sometimes longed to be back in his prison cell.

Many years ago, someone called me and said, 'Could you take Richard Wurmbrand to Cambridge?' Sadly, I had too many engagements but I would love to have done so. He had had a letter threatening his life and he was not going to travel by public transport for safety reasons. I asked, 'What does he want to go for?', and was told he was going to challenge (then) Canon Montefiore in Cambridge because it was in that man's church that the World Congress of Faiths had met a few weeks before, and it was in that man's church that Montefiore called Jesus a homosexual, which is nigh blasphemy. Wurmbrand, who had suffered physically in eastern Europe, was the man who was going to challenge this person to preach the truth in the West. Does that not humble you? This is the battle we fight today, and we must say very clearly and lovingly: 'We are not altering the faith for the intellectuals of today. There is only one gospel that saves!'

2

HOW DID THE WORLD GET INTO THE EARLY CHURCH?

We are attempting to cover an immense amount of ground in a brief survey. The purpose is to see the unfolding purpose of God, and how things that we know only too well actually came about. In the previous chapter we considered how the church captured the world (over the first four hundred years) by winning a physical battle over suffering, a mental battle with heresy and a spiritual battle over other religions. Something important to be added is this: the Christians won that battle because they outlived, out-thought, and out-died everyone else. That is not my statement but that of the Baptist scholar T. R. Glover.

In this and the next chapter we now move to a more unhappy and serious subject, namely how the world captured the church.

There is a painting from the Middle Ages that portrays the church as a lifeboat. In a tossing sea, the Christians in the lifeboat are reaching out to pluck from the waves people who are drowning. Now that is quite a good picture of the church. It is a lifeboat and it has gone into the world, responding to the cry 'SOS' – 'save our souls'. The lifeboat must be in the sea, but if the sea gets into the lifeboat, then there is real trouble. The church must be in the world but when the world gets into the church, then it is finished and it sinks. The story of the next thousand years is about how the sea got into the lifeboat, how the world got into the church.

In this chapter we look at how the world got into the church in the early period from about AD 100 to 400, so we will revisit the period we have already covered. Even with all that victory, the world was beginning to get into the church. Later, in Chapter 3, we will look at the period AD 400 to 1000, often referred to as the Dark Ages, before we tackle the Middle Ages (1000–1500), bringing us within just a year or two of Martin Luther.

First, then, how did the world get into the church in the first four hundred years, when there were martyrs like those we have already looked at, when there were great preachers, when the battle was being won? Four things happened during those first four centuries that began to water down the church of Jesus Christ:

- Regional bishops;
- A 'Magic' view of the sacraments;
- Established religion;
- Nominal membership.

REGIONAL BISHOPS

In the New Testament period every church had a number of bishops to itself. They were called elders, or bishops, or presbyters. The names refer to the same office – spiritual leaders. So bishops in the New Testament were the same as some churches call elders today.

In the next stage, each church reduced its bishops to one. Then, later, there was only one bishop to many churches and the leadership was being concentrated in fewer hands.

You can't find that in the New Testament. It didn't happen for the first hundred years of the Christian church, but the change took place in the second century. Now there emerged men of considerable power and influence – not many bishops to one church, but many churches to one bishop. This departure from the divine order in the New Testament was quite clearly one of the first things that began to spoil and to change the character of the church. This change, incidentally, copied the Roman Empire, with its governors.

A 'MAGIC' VIEW OF THE SACRAMENTS

Consider baptism. Instead of being an outward sign and seal of the spiritual washing away of sins, it began to be believed that the actual water and the use of the right formula saved a person from their sin, whatever their age; and that, in fact, if you sinned after your baptism you undid it, and you couldn't get it again, so you had better not! So they decided that they had better not be baptized until they were on their death bed. After all, if you get baptized before you are dying, there is a big risk of sinning afterwards, and undoing the good work of washing away your sin, and quite literally, people began putting off baptism, until the doctors said, 'There is no hope'. And then they rushed for the minister and said, 'Baptise!' But then others said, 'Look, we might have a baby who dies. We would much rather have the baptism right at the beginning of life, and get the baby's sins washed away. We don't want our baby in hell!' Both these views were superstitious and magical.

Unfortunately, it was the view of infant baptism which prevailed. So, after about 150 years, babies began to be baptised, a practice that has persisted to this day, not in the majority of churches in the world, but probably coming up to half. That practice meant that many began to say, 'I'm Christian' who had simply been 'Christened'. That eroded the church of Jesus Christ.

Similarly, the Lord's Supper was treated magically. It was in the first four hundred years that they began to think that the bread actually was the flesh of Christ, and that the wine actually was the blood, and therefore since his actual flesh and blood were being offered, it was in fact a sacrifice, and therefore the minister handling the bread and wine must in fact be a priest.

ESTABLISHED RELIGION

When the Emperor went to church, you can imagine everybody else did too. When the Emperor Constantine said, 'From now on, there is only one official religion, and that is Christianity', you can imagine everybody climbed on the band-wagon and it became fashionable. It became respectable to go to the church of the established religion of the country. I believe that an established religion produces fashionable and respectable Christianity. It is bound to and I cannot find it in the New Testament.

NOMINAL MEMBERSHIP

So nominal membership came into the church. At the end of the second century, one writer said this: 'About [AD] 50 he was of the church who had received baptism and the Holy Spirit and called Jesus "Lord", but about 180 who acknowledged the rule of faith (that is, the creed), the New Testament canon and the authority of the bishops.'

In other words, people were joining for other reasons, than that they believed in Jesus and had received his Holy Spirit. It was now *an institution*

Now, of course, at every stage when the church went wrong there were protests. The protests in the first four hundred years were two movements called Montanism and monasticism. They were both protests against a church that was getting wealthy and worldly, and was getting filled up with people who had never even been converted.

MONTANISM

This arose in what we now call Turkey, in Asia Minor. A man called Montanus noticed that in scores of church members there was no trace of the Holy Spirit, and so he sought afresh the Holy Spirit of God – and there was a revival in Asia Minor. Now I think if you wanted to know who they were most like today, they were Pentecostals. They re-discovered the Holy Spirit of God, and the gifts of the Spirit came back into the church through Montanism. The life came back into the worship. Vigour and reality came back through this Pentecostal protest against the deadness of the church and against the worldliness of its members.

With a tremendous emphasis on the return of Christ, with an insistence that nobody be a member of the church unless they could profess and possess a real faith in Christ, with holiness and fasting, with a serious Christian life, this Pentecostal revival challenged the existing church.

But the bishops opposed it very severely. I think you can guess why. The tragedy is that, as so often, this first Pentecostal movement in history went wrong. It went wrong because these people would not have teaching. They wanted the 'heat' without the 'light'. You have got to have both. Light without heat is very cold. Heat without light is too hot. They wouldn't listen to teaching from the scriptures on how to exercise spiritual gifts. Particularly it was the women of this movement who went wrong. They began to produce prophetesses and others who were unbalanced, frenzied and fanatical, and who would not be controlled or taught.

The tragedy is that that first Pentecostal revival ended in fanaticism and fizzled out. The protest came to nothing. I think that is something every Pentecostal revival needs to know. We can learn from history. It arose as a good thing, as a protest against the deadness of the churches, as the present Pentecostal movement arose over a century ago, for precisely the same reason, in England. But, all the time, such revival needs to be balanced with teaching, with the balanced use of gifts, with the scriptural brakes on the thing, or it becomes frenzied and fanatical.

MONASTICISM

The other protest (some years later in that early period) was very different. There were certain Christians who said: this church is so worldly, so dead, that the only hope of re-discovering Christianity is to get out of the church as well as out of the world.

Now some of the early ones decided to do it on their own. They were hermits. It is the strangest tale. There was for example the first: St. Anthony. He decided that he would never be a real Christian until he got into the middle of the desert. The trouble was that, when he got there, a lot of other Christians thought they would join him, and he didn't want that. Above all, he found that his temptations were just as worldly sitting in a cave in the desert as they had been in the church.

There was the even more peculiar hermit called Simeon Stylites. He built himself a pillar 60 feet high, a yard across at the top. He went up there and lived there for some 60 years. He even stood on one leg for a year to try, as a protest, to tell the church that Christianity is something tough. So there he was, up the pole in more senses than one, covered in ulcers and worms, in a most frightful state, and poor old Simeon Stylites has gone down into history as one who tried to recover the true asceticism of the Christian faith, and the true vigour and self-discipline of it, in a worldly church.

More successful than the hermits, were those who started communities of Christians. A man called Benedict started this movement. On Monte Casino, half way between Rome and Naples, this man gathered around him a group of real Christians, who realised the church was so worldly, so dead that they couldn't do anything with it, and they said: We will come together and live together as Christians. We will not be wealthy, we will be poor; we will not be lustful, we will be celibate; we will not be rebellious, we will be obedient. They adopted the three-fold vows of poverty, chastity and obedience. It was run on the lines of a Roman soldiers' garrison. This monastery was a protest against a worldly church.

The tragedy is that this protest went wrong, just as certainly as the other. For Christ did not mean us to live the Christian life away from everybody else. And later these monks, who started with a good intention of re-discovering Christianity, became so wrapped up in their own salvation, so introverted, that they were isolated from the world and the church.

Furthermore, the monks, I am afraid, produced the idea that there were two sorts of Christians – two standards and two levels. There are second class Christians who get married and first class Christians who don't. There are second class Christians who live in the world, and there are first class Christians who live out of it. But that is not the teaching of Jesus. Our Lord was not a monk. He didn't withdraw from society. He lived a pure life in the society, and he told his disciples to be in the world without being of it. So this protest was not the right one, but it was sincere.

3

THE DARK AGES
AD 400 – 1000

THE FALL OF ROME

In the year 410 there was a catastrophe. The Barbarians from the north pressed down on the city of Rome. The Vandals (as we still call people who destroy everything in their tracks) came, the Franks came, the Huns, the Goths – these 'Barbarians' (so called because of their war-cry, 'Barbar, Barbar'!)

So the Rome of that day fell. The Romans left Britain in that year, to go back to defend the city, but they were not able to do so. As soon as the Romans got out of Britain, the Jutes, the Angles and the Saxons came charging in here and they destroyed Christianity in England and in south-east Scotland, so Christianity, which had been brought by Roman soldiers and which was in England within the first four hundred years, vanished when the Romans left Britain. The Anglo-Saxons came in and just conquered it all.

When Rome fell, it seemed as if this was the end

of civilisation. Jerome, writing in Jerusalem said, 'The human race is included in the ruins.' It was puzzling to many that whilst Rome had survived hundreds of years as a pagan empire, now as a Christian one it had collapsed.

ST. AUGUSTINE

But there was one man who thought it through and came up with the most incredible statement, namely that it was the best thing that had ever happened. His name was Augustine, and you can buy his books on airport bookstalls even today. You would recognise some of the things this great man said: 'Our hearts are restless and they can find no rest until they find their rest in thee' – I suppose the most quoted prayer in history. It was Augustine who prayed, 'Give me chastity, but not just yet'. It was Augustine who said, 'Love and do what you like.' He had more influence on church history than any other man after the apostle Paul. Born in North Africa, he went as a student to the university at Carthage, got into the wrong crowd of young men, and pretty soon had a concubine, by whom he had a son. He lived in an illegal relationship with his concubine for some twenty years. He had a pagan father, but a very godly and saintly mother who prayed for him with tears every day.

Later, because of his brilliant mind and academic career, he was invited to be a Professor of Rhetoric in Milan University. There he heard the saintly Bishop Ambrose, whose mortal remains I have looked upon. Under the preaching of Ambrose, this young man Augustine, with his brilliant mind, but with his thoroughly profligate living, was brought into a tremendous conviction of uncertainty and sin. One day, sitting in a garden, weeping over the mess he had made of his life, he heard a child's voice, a boy's voice over the garden wall, saying, 'Take up and read, take up and read.' He never knew who that boy was. But he noticed a scroll on the seat by him, and he took it up and read it, and it was Paul's letter to the Romans! Augustine read it through, and the light dawned. When he walked out in the street afterwards, the woman he lived with saw him and he ran away from her. She ran after him and said, 'Augustine, it is I, it is I', and he replied, shouting over his shoulder, 'But it is not I, it is not I.'

Gradually he got his life straightened out and he began to write. You can read the whole story of his conversion in his *Confessions*. It was when Augustine was in his middle age that Rome fell and the whole world seemed to collapse about his ears. He began thinking about this, and finally wrote another important book (he wrote many!) *City of God*, in which he said that it was a good thing that the pagan city of Rome had collapsed, because now the city of God could replace it. It was good that an earthly empire had come to an end, because the heavenly empire could be established. This book brought hope and new life to many people. It brought them to see that there was a city of God that still survived when the city of men had gone.

That was the trouble, because people began to ask: what is this city of God? Is it a visible thing? Or an invisible thing? Is it an earthly or a heavenly city? At this point, Augustine led many people into a misunderstanding through this second book. The funny thing is that centuries later, in the Reformation, Protestants said, 'We follow Augustine' and the Roman Catholics said, 'We follow Augustine'! But the Protestants were following his *Confessions*, and the Roman Catholics were following his *City of God*. For this is what happened. The church said, 'Well, if that is the truth, then the church is now the new empire', and one of the first results of this was the rise of the Roman bishop to the position of emperor.

Now in those days, there was a great debate about the word 'pope'. It means, essentially, 'father'. In spite of the fact that Jesus had said, 'Don't ever call anyone on earth father. You have one Father in heaven', they began to call the local priest, 'father'. Then they called the regional bishops, 'father'. Then a number of great bishops including those of Jerusalem, Alexandria, Constantinople and Rome began to claim the title. The Bishop of Rome said, 'Now look, the city of Rome has gone but I am the emperor now. I am the chief bishop, and from now on, you only call me Pope, you only call me father', and the papacy as we know it came into being.

The interesting thing is the Pope adopted the titles and even the robes of the Roman Emperor!

He adopted the title *Pontifex Maximus* – otherwise known today as the Pontiff. It is the Roman Emperor's title. Augustine's idea was mistaken and people thought the church was the new empire. It was to have its emperor, and its robes and ceremonies. It must have its throne. The Pope became a king.

Now, of course, you would imagine that Christians were having none of that. The French Christians wouldn't have it. The Irish Christians wouldn't have it. The Welsh Christians wouldn't have it and the Scottish Christians wouldn't have it. But I'm afraid the English Christians did.

At one time it looked as if the British Isles would be caught between those who believed Christianity didn't have a Pope and those who believed it did. St. Columba went from Ireland to Iona and into Scotland, and led Scotland to Christ. Then down came Aidan to the island of Lindisfarne from which he evangelised Northumberland. You can still see the ruins of St Aidan's church there, on the little island. So this non-papal Celtic Christianity came through Ireland and Scotland into northern England. But later the Pope said, 'We've got to get England. We've got to get those Angles.' He sent a missionary, another Augustine, who landed on the island of Thanet and later arrived in Canterbury. The two sorts of Christianity, Celtic and Roman, had a famous meeting at Whitby. You can see the ruins above Whitby harbour where they met.

There, in the year 660, papal Christianity met

Celtic Christianity, and the tragedy is that papal Christianity won and the British Isles came under the papal throne. Scotland even changed its patron saint from St John to St Andrew. The whole situation was changed.

The other great group of Christians who would have none of this were the churches of the eastern part of the Mediterranean: those of Greece, Asia Minor, Syria and Egypt. They said, 'We are not acknowledging this. This is not Scriptural, that there should be one "papa", one father of the whole church. This is not New Testament.' They began a split which was finally completed by the year 1054, that kept the Eastern and the Western churches apart until the 1960s. Only in the twentieth century did the Eastern and the Western churches begin to talk together. For a thousand years they split over this very thing. Of course, they have still to resolve the matter.

So the church became an empire, and the man who did it most was, of course, Pope Gregory. Then there was Leo the Great. He claimed to be Peter's successor. One of the most incredible things happened. In the year 850, the Pope said, 'I have discovered certain documents which go back to the very first century which prove that Peter appointed the first Pope, and he appointed the second and he appointed the third', and so it went on. We now know, and the Roman church now knows, that those documents were a forgery. They are known as the forged *decretals*, yet the papacy was built on a forgery. There was also another forgery called the *Donation of Constantine*, which claimed that all of Italy belonged to the Pope. The Pope discovered this forged document and said, 'There! All Italy belongs to me!' This is the kind of foundation on which that whole structure was based, and even Rome knows that it is today, and yet still persists in claiming it. So Roman power was extending.

CHARLEMAGNE

In 742 a man was born whose dream was that the empire of Rome should be restored and put back on the map, with himself as Emperor, with the Pope beneath him. His name, Charlemagne, strikes a chill when you hear it. This ruthless man said, 'We will have a Roman Empire back again and its head will not be a pope but an emperor.' Charlemagne saved the Pope's life twice, once from the Barbarians and once from the crowds in Rome who were angry with him. The Pope said, 'You have saved my life twice; what will you have me do for you?' The Emperor said, 'Christmas Day, crown me Emperor!'

In the year 800, on Christmas Day, in the largest church in Rome, in the Christmas morning service, the Pope crowned the King of the Franks: 'Charlemagne, the Emperor of the Holy Roman Empire'. A thousand years later, the Holy Roman Empire still existed.

We have come full circle. The empire of Rome collapsed in 410. The church took over the empire.

Then in 800 the Emperor took over the empire from the church. It looked as if the whole thing was back again to where it started.

Charlemagne did some good things and he did some bad things. He stopped the clergymen having concubines, and visiting taverns and going hunting, and he founded schools, amongst some of his good works. Amongst the bad works were that he forbade clergy ever to marry, and it is to Charlemagne that we owe the celibacy of the Roman priesthood.

Charlemagne had an idea of a kingdom in which he and the Pope were partners, with himself as the senior partner in the business. He coined the term 'Christendom' (Christ–en–dom, meaning the kingdom which would be Christian under the emperor. The word is an idea that has persisted until this day, and there are still some who hope that one day there will be a Christendom that will be Christ's kingdom.

PROTESTS

The church, because it had become powerful and wealthy, was corrupt. Once again, I want to tell you about the protests that arose. We now had a church that had a Pope as its head, a church that venerated images, a church that taught people that they would be saved by 'doing pilgrimage' and 'penance'. This church was telling people all sorts of things that you cannot find in the New Testament. The protests came in the East and in the North.

It came in the East, from two developments.

The first was the greatest judgment there has ever been on the Christian church, which was the rise of Islam. Now I have lived in Arabia and I have seen something of this religion. Let me tell you a bit about it.

Mohammed was born in 571 in a town called Mecca which was the centre of idolatrous superstition for the Arab race. In the middle of Mecca was a huge square building, covered with black curtains and in it was a sacred stone, the Ka'ba, a meteorite that had fallen from the sky. But there was much other superstition and idolatry in Arabia. This man, Mohammed, grew up with the idolatry and superstition of the Arabs and he was revolted and disgusted by it, so, listen to this! He turned, first to the Jew and then to the Christians and said, 'Have you got the true religion?' The tragedy was that Mohammed never met a converted Christian! The tragedy that he never saw real Christianity of the New Testament kind! All he saw were priests in vestments and images and crucifixes and he said, 'That's as idolatrous as the Arab's religion.' Now if only Mohammed had met one true Christian at the end of the sixth century, but he didn't so he said, 'Right. I'm going to seek a new religion that is pure.' And he turned away from this wretched perverted Christianity which by this time was all that he could find.

So he married a wealthy widow and he spent years in the desert and in the desert he says he was spoken to, and a voice said, 'There is no God but

Allah and Mohammed is his prophet.' He began to preach this. Through an amanuensis or amanuenses he wrote down what he heard in his visions in a book – the Koran. He was persecuted and he had to flee to Medina in the year 622 and that is the date from which the Arabs take their calendar. He came back to Mecca and he imposed the new religion on the place – with an army! From then on, everybody had to pray to Mecca. By a religion of good works, by fasting, by praying five times a day, by fasting during Ramadan, by making pilgrimage to Mecca, by giving alms to the poor, it was taught that you could get to heaven.

Mohammedanism swept Christianity out of the Mediterranean. It swept Christianity out of the North African coast. It swept Christianity out of the Holy Land itself, out of Jerusalem, out of the place where Jesus died. It swept up through Spain and up through Asia Minor. It swept into France and got as far as the gates of Lyons. It swept into Eastern Europe and got as far as Vienna and it looked as if Mohammedanism was going to crush Christianity in a gigantic pincer movement. It is the greatest judgement God has ever allowed to come on the Christian church and it was deserved. Christianity vanished over most of the Mediterranean coast.

But 'so far and no further'. God was not going to have Christianity wiped out altogether and he stopped them at Lyons and Vienna and they withdrew to their present boundaries – mainly the North African coast and up to Turkey. Because, at this time, all over Europe there were little groups of Christians meeting around the Word of God. They saw that the official church was corrupt and they simply met together in tiny groups. They read the Bible and said, 'We will worship God in simplicity. We will worship together. We don't need priests. We've got Jesus, our High Priest. We don't need a Pope. We've got a Father in heaven. We don't need all this paraphernalia. We just need the Word of God and the Holy Spirit', and so they met.

Now we hardly know anything about them because they were so persecuted that even the records of their history are destroyed. I wonder how many have ever heard of a group of people called the Bogomils. They were a group of people who met around the Word of God all over Europe. They met primarily in Bulgaria and Bosnia. And the word 'Bogomil' is the Bulgarian word meaning 'friends' – friends of God.

There were the Paulicians who met in Armenia and Thracia and Asia Minor. There were the Catharia – a name which means 'the pure ones', the same as the later word 'Puritan' – and they met in the Balkans.

I used to think in my simplicity that, for a thousand years, the only churches were the Roman church and the Eastern churches, but this is not true. I was thrilled to discover that all through those centuries there were groups of simple Christians who met around the Word of God in local churches. They paid for it with their lives, but they met and the flame of faith was kept alight for succeeding generations.

4

THE MIDDLE AGES
AD 1000 – 1500

We call AD 1000–1500 the 'Middle Ages' because it is the period between the 'Dark Ages' and the 'Modern Age'.

HILDEBRAND
This monk became Pope and he didn't like being 'number two'. There was now a restored Roman Empire with a new Emperor, but the Pope was number two. Hildebrand decided that the Pope should be number one. I am putting that very simply but it is precisely what happened – and Hildebrand achieved it. He did many good things. He cut out some of the simony in the church ['simony' means buying ecclesiastical posts]. He cut out many things that were wrong, but he did it because he believed the Pope should be in control of everything, including kings. The battle between Hildebrand and the Emperor, Henry IV by this time, was settled in a most dramatic and

terrible way. Henry IV defied Hildebrand and said, 'I'm number one.' Hildebrand said, 'You are not! Let the people decide.' The people decided that Hildebrand was. Away in the Alps, the Pope met Henry IV who came from Northern Europe. The Pope was in a mountain house and he kept the Emperor waiting outside in the snow, bare-footed, for three days, before he would speak to him. In this way, Hildebrand very definitely put the Emperor in a secondary place.

From then and for the next five hundred years, the Pope is the most influential figure, and the Papacy is the power that controls the Western world. The church is now the empire again, and it was this Pope that started the symbol for the Popes which one of my children wore on his school uniform, much to my disgust – the crossed keys of Chalfont St Peter. One of those keys is the key of sacred authority over the church and the other is the key of secular authority over the state. The crossed keys of St Peter which were part of our local community crest are, in fact, the claim of Hildebrand to be 'top dog' over church and state.

This put the physical force of armies at the church's disposal, and because Hildebrand thought this way, he began to use force to establish the kingdom of Christ. Never was a greater mistake made.

CRUSADES TO THE HOLY LAND

The first outcome of this idea that force is valid for the church to use was the Crusades. By this time the holy places, including Jerusalem, were in the hands of Muslims. The Pope, encouraged by others, decided that the church would fight its way in and capture the Holy Land for Christ. The first crusade was born in 1095. It was Hildebrand's idea but he died before it could be done. Even during his lifetime, though, some people were setting off. Just as people today have a craze for marching ('walk so many miles and you sponsor me', and so on), that was considered *the* cause to march for then! There were walks in aid of this all over the place. You walked, because you were crusading. You wore a 'cross' on your shoulders, and this was called a 'crux-aid', and from that we get the word 'crusade'. You marched behind these banners or with these things on your shoulders, as epaulettes.

The first crusade was pulled together by an unkempt, uncouth, fanatical preacher called Peter the Hermit. He set off with 600,000 men, and only a tenth of them arrived. Most of them died in the high mountains of Turkey. But they got there. They took Jerusalem, and they pillaged it. They raped the women, and they established the so-called 'rule of Christ' in Jerusalem, by slaughtering all the Saracens of that city. Now is that Christian? Of course not. They were misled, and thousands of people thought this was what the church was meant to be, an earthly empire, establishing itself by force. There were incentives. They were offered absolution from their sins if they would go and fight for Christ. They were offered indulgences, so many years off purgatory, which was now believed in. They were told that their debts would be cancelled by law, if they went. They were told that there was pardon for criminals who would leave prison to go and fight. You can imagine the kind of motley crew that resulted.

Philip of France was caught up in it, as was King Richard (Coeur-de-Lion) of England. Eight times crusaders set off to go and take that place. You can still see the ruins of Crusader castles all over the Holy Land – Acre, Mount Hermon, there they are. It was the greatest disaster there has ever been.

One of the crusades was a children's crusade, and two thousand little mites set off to march across Europe to try and get the Holy Land back for Jesus. Not one of them ever arrived. The Pope said, 'You will have food miraculously provided for you by angels if you go,' but the food never came and the angels never appeared. It is the most incredible story which you ought to read if you want to understand the background of the Reformation.

What was the basic failure? The answer is that it was thought you established the kingdom of Christ by physical force.

The Knights of St John of Jerusalem, the Knights Templar, orders of Christian knights were founded. It all sounded grand, and worth marching for. It caught the imagination of young people and off they went, by the thousand, to their death.

The last crusade was an utter failure. At the flat-topped mountain of the Horns of Hittin, the last crusader army died of thirst, besieged by the Saracens. So in 1270 Europe breathed a sigh of relief because the Pope called the whole thing off. It is one of the saddest stories in the histories of the church. It achieved nothing, indeed it did worse than nothing.

From using force outside the church, the Pope now decided to use force inside the church and began another dreadful chapter.

THE INQUISITION

I dare not go into a description of the things done in the name of Christ. The bishops refused to run this dreadful machine of cruelty, malice and suspicion to force people to toe the Christian line, but the Dominicans took it up and for many years, many people went in fear of their lives through that dreadful thing, the Inquisition.

All the way through, what was wrong was that the church thought of itself as an earthly empire in which it was valid to use force to establish the cause of Christ. We now know this is not the way to do it. We know that the church must use no other force but love, and must never force anyone, except through love and through preaching the gospel, to accept Christ. Of course, this kind of corruption soon turns in on itself. 'Power tends to corrupt,' said Lord Acton, 'and absolute power tends to corrupt absolutely.' (By the way, that is the right quotation of his words.) And it corrupted. Very soon the Pope was two Popes, and there were two fighting for the throne. Then three Popes, and people wondered what on earth the world was coming to. There was a Pope in Avignon (*Sur le pont, d'Avignon*). There was the Pope. There was the pontiff at Avignon, not just the '*pont*'! There he was! And there was a Pope somewhere else, there was a Pope in Rome. Who is Pope now? You see, this kind of behaviour soon leads to this kind of disintegration. They managed to pull the Papacy together, but then the corruption began to come further down.

The monasteries became corrupt. They became too wealthy. The bishops became too powerful. The parishes became corrupt, and the practices of ordinary Christian religion were corrupt. There were prayers to Mary. We were never told to pray to Mary. She was a human being like the rest of us. There were prayers for the dead. There were prayers to the saints. There was the doctrine which caused the greatest fear: the doctrine of purgatory – how many years you go through suffering after you die. There was the doctrine of the 'mass', the 'sacrifice', so called, of the Lord's Supper, offered by the priest. There was confession to the priest. There were indulgences, so that for a sum of money you could buy so many years off purgatory. There were pilgrimages. There was the worship of relics. There were images in worship. None of this was in the New Testament. But when such corruption sets in, everything seems to go wrong. When such power and wealth come to the church, it is not long before worship and other things are destroyed.

What was the basic fault behind all this? What was wrong? I will tell you in one sentence: the church had begun to think she was Christ – and still does.

I asked a leading priest, 'Is this still true?' And he said, 'Yes, that will not change.' I was asking about the Vatican Council and discussing it with him. I said, 'Look, my one difference, my one problem is this: that I do not believe the church is Christ, and I do not believe that she is prophet, priest and king. I believe that Jesus is.'

He told me very frankly, 'We will not discuss that, nor will the Vatican Council because that will never change.'

Here is the basic fault: if I believe that I am the prophet to the world, then I can tell the world what to believe and I can say, infallibly, what is true. If I am the world's priest, I can say, 'You've got to come to my sacraments, you've got to confess to me if you are ever to find salvation.' And if I think I am the king of the world, then I will establish my authority as widely as I can.

It is a confusion between the head and the body of the church. The head is divine. The body is human. It is Christ who is the head, and it is he who is the prophet, priest and king. The church is not. That is the basic difference between Protestantism and

Catholicism; it is as big a difference today as it ever was, and there is no change in the situation. Not an inch has moved in this regard.

It was during the Middle Ages that the Papacy began to think of itself as prophet, priest and king and as the vicar of Christ on earth, so that when the Pope speaks from his seat, it is Christ who is speaking. Now that is the fundamental thing. I say it in love, but that is still the issue. It hasn't changed one inch and it is still the biggest question to be faced. A book that makes this clear is by an Italian, Vitoria de Subilia, entitled *The Problem of Catholicism.* I have loaned it to priests and they have told me quite frankly when they have read it, 'That is a good book. That is the best Protestant book there is on Rome.' That is what the reviews in the Roman Catholic press have indicated. One comment was: 'It is the best Protestant book on Rome there has been and it's absolutely accurate on what we believe and we are not changing what we do believe and this is it.'

The church is not Christ, therefore the church is not King; the city of God is something whose builder and maker is God, not man. Christ said, 'I will build my church'. He didn't say *you* build it. Christ is the head of the church and no-one else is the head, and no-one else must be. Even in a local church, the minister can try to be head of the church; the elders can try to be head of the church. But my prayer is that the government of each church shall be upon *his* shoulder and that Christ shall be the head. There is no other and there can never be. When the church begins to behave as if it is Christ, then these things come in.

Now I am happy to say that there were protests, and all through the Middle Ages, from 1000 to 1500, there were people who said, 'This is not true! This is not Christianity. This is not what Jesus meant to happen.' These little groups were known under various names. I just want to mention four to give you some idea.

There were the Beghards, from the Netherlands. They were just people who met around the book and said, 'Christ is the head of our church'. Then there were the Waldenses, named after the Waldensian Valley in northern Italy where they began. The Waldenses said, 'We believe that this book, the scriptures, tell us what Jesus meant the church to be.' They went to the Pope and they said, 'This is what we see. Could we be recognised as validly part of the church if we practise this book?' Could they have done more? They wanted to stay in the Roman church, but they wanted to follow this book. The Pope said, 'No, if you do what you intend to do, we will persecute you.' And they did. The Waldensians fled from one valley to another.

The next group were the Albigensians in southern France. They read the Bible and said, 'Now we see what the church is meant to be like and what Christians are meant to be like.' I am afraid the most bloody campaign that was ever promulgated from the Papacy was against these dear people, the Albigensians. But there were two Spanish noblemen, sent by the Pope, to put them to death. They returned to the Pope and said, 'But these are good Christians. They're not criminals. They're not fighting you. They want to be in the church. They want to practise their understanding of the scripture.' Those two men, one of whom was named Dominic, said, 'We will try and bring this within the church' – and they started the Dominicans (the Order of Preachers). They were a copy of the Albigensians. It is a tragedy that, later, the Dominicans became so corrupted that they were willing to do the Inquisition.

There were others. There was the Brethren of the Common Life in Germany. All of these were independent of the Roman Catholic hierarchy. They based everything on the Bible, in the people's language, and they were all persecuted to the death. The true church has always been persecuted.

Now among those inside the church who saw this as well were people who withdrew and saw it privately. Bernard of Clairvaux was one of these. He was a very serious young man, although in his youth he had been the ring-leader of a real gang of thieves. But, after he had been a prisoner-of-war for two years in the wars of Italy, he came to himself. He realised that he was wasting his life, and he became a serious man. The son of a French baron, he withdrew from his riches and went with twelve friends into a valley full of robbers in the southern part of France. There he lived a terribly poor life, eating cooked beech leaves and herbs. He got his friends up at two o'clock every morning for prayer. He wouldn't let them stop work until eight o'clock at night, and they built a community in the valley of Clairvaux. Bernard became one of the most powerful Christians in Europe. He even chose one Pope. He did it without any office, without any money, without any material or psychological force whatsoever. He did it because he was the great Christian that he was. People came to him from all over and asked his advice. Then he went out and preached all over. Bernard of Clairvaux became a very great man, an influential man, because of his moral character. He was later called the Pope maker because he put Innocent III on the papal throne. In private, he loved Jesus. Martin Luther once said, 'Of all the monks and priests of history I have the highest esteem for Bernard of Clairvaux.' Alas, in public, he felt bound to support the Papacy and someone has wisely said, 'He set back the Reformation by at least two centuries' – and I am afraid this man with his wonderful private love of the Lord, publicly set back what might have happened.

Francis, a near contemporary, born in the little town of Assisi, was a man you will have heard of. He was brought up to face life by meeting a beggar, a leper, in the street, and he walked right past that leper, on the other side. As he walked past he thought, 'What sort of a man am I, to walk away from my fellow man?' – and he went back and kissed the leper. Francis then began to be serious about life; he sought Christ, and he found Christ. Francis gathered around him a number of friends who went out, two by two, in utter poverty, preaching the gospel, winning people for Christ. Although he is better remembered for his remarkable way with animals and birds (and his love of nature was unique), Francis ought to be remembered as the first missionary to the Muslims. Risking his life, he went to the Sultan himself – the head of the Muslims – to preach the gospel of Jesus Christ. Instead of going with an army of 600,000 soldiers to fight them, Francis went alone, in poverty, to preach the love of Jesus.

These men stand out. Francis and his followers wore grey robes and became known as the Grey Friars. You will find the name Greyfriars in city streets. The Dominicans wore black robes so they were known as Black Friars and you will find Blackfriars commemorated in streets in London. So the Greyfriars and the Blackfriars tried to bring back the simple Christian life into the church. But the sad story is that they, too, failed and became corrupt, and the Franciscans became professional beggars and the Dominicans, as we have noted, ran the Inquisition.

The whole situation was crying out for someone to say what the truth was, and to say it so well that everybody would hear and understand. A man called Arnold of Brescia in 1150 began to say that wealth and worldly power should not be in the church's hands. But alas, Bernard of Clairvaux opposed him and got him quietened. Then came a man called Marsilius, a medical doctor. Reading his Bible, he said, 'The Bible is the standard of the church, and no other, and bishops and popes are human inventions.' But he was silenced. An Englishman who was a professor in the University of Paris, a man called William of Ockham, said this, and he was silenced.

Finally, it fell to the lot of a Yorkshireman to be what is called the 'Morning Star' of the Reformation. The Morning star is one you can still see as the sun is coming up. He came to Oxford as a brilliant student, became a professor at Oxford, travelled around a great deal, and was nicknamed 'Doctor Evangelicus'. You can guess why. His name was John Wycliffe and he re-discovered the Bible, I suppose, more than anyone else, until Martin Luther. He got it across and he protested against Papal abuse.

There were five decrees of the Papacy against him. They were called 'bulls' in those days. He was taken to Canterbury and put on trial, but he turned to the scriptures, the only law of the church, and he said, 'I am going to put this Bible, from the Latin, into English. I am going to cause the ploughboys to know this book.' John Wycliffe painstakingly translated the Bible, knowing that if you can put it into the hands of ordinary men and women you have given them the answer for all corruption in the church. So he worked away at this and he achieved it.

He gathered around him a group of preachers who used to walk around quite simply in the villages, with Wycliffe's translation of the Bible and they would preach in the market square – they were good singers too. They sang the gospel, and wherever you'll find the gospel really preached, you will find it sung too. They were called 'those who sang lullabies' – Lollards. (Lollard and lullaby are the same word.) Something was happening that was going to lead to tremendous things.

You might visit Amersham. Go up Station Road, turn left through the houses, into the field. There is a monument to people who were burned alive by their own children, who were forced to light the bonfires, and who burnt their parents to death. Why? Because they were caught in Amersham Woods reading their Bibles, and it was the result of Wycliffe and the Lollards that that happened, and that the monument is up there. You should know this. It happened in the Chilterns, and Wycliffe went everywhere. The interesting thing is that he died preaching peacefully as the Rector of Lutterworth (now just off the M1, south of Leicester). I went into that church in Lutterworth. It would have broken John Wycliffe's heart. It was more Roman than Rome. I could hardly see for the incense, from the high liturgy – there it was. There was the place where Wycliffe preached the Word and condemned the corruption that there was in the church.

Now he was at Oxford. And there was another

university in Europe that had a close link with Oxford, namely the University of Prague. The Rector of Prague was a poor peasant boy who had risen by sheer hard work to be the Rector of the University of Prague. His name was John as well. – John (Jan) Huss. Huss heard of Wycliffe and began to read his books and started to preach the same thing in Prague. John Huss was finally arrested and the Pope condemned him to be burned to death. And the Hussites were put to death.

When word got back to England that the Pope had burned John Huss, do you know what they did? Church authorities went to Lutterworth, dug up the body of John Wycliffe and burnt it on a bonfire, and the ashes they threw into the River Swift at Lutterworth. Someone said about that: 'As the River Swift will bear the ashes into the River Avon and as the River Avon will bear the ashes into the River Severn, and as the River Severn will bear the ashes into the channels around our shores, and as those channels will bear those ashes to the oceans, so will the teachings of John Wycliffe spread throughout the world.' That was an amazing prophecy.

Now we are on the brink of something exciting. Don't you get excited? You can see that this could not go on for ever. Such an abuse of the church of Christ could not be tolerated by men and women. They were beginning to see, and what was enabling them to see was that they were beginning to read the Bible in their own language. Wherever the

Bible goes, it will do this. It will put things right.

Now I come to my last point: the other thing that caused the Reformation was not just the abuse of the church, it was that men were entering an age of discovery and they were beginning to get new ideas.

This was true in the *material* realm. Christopher Columbus was discovering America, Copernicus was discovering how the earth went round the sun, and not the other way round, Galileo was putting the telescope to his blinding eyes and he was looking at the stars. It was beginning to be the age of science, when men would question things.

Furthermore, it was a new age of discovery in mental realms: there was re-discovery of Greek literature and art. In Raphael's paintings you will see the re-discovery of ancient culture coming out because Constantinople had fallen to the Turks and the Greek treasures of art had been swept away into Italy and the new art and the new learning were being spread.

The printing press had been invented and that helped the new learning. One of the great new scholars was a man called Erasmus. Among many other things, he began to re-discover the Greek New Testament and the Hebrew Old Testament. It was a re-discovery of old things as well as new. So Erasmus said, 'I am going to get such an accurate New Testament that even women, Scots, Irish, Turks and Saracens will be able to get the message!' All due apologies, but that is what he said. So he produced an accurate New Testament, and instead of the word 'penance' appeared the word 'repentance' and many things were put right that were wrong in the Bible that they had.

In all this tremendous discovery of mental things, of art and music, of sculpture, all that we call the Renaissance, they discovered that if people are intellectually better, they are not morally better. It was the age when the Popes were filling their Palace with art treasures and it was the age of Caesar and Locretia Borgia, the most immoral Papal family there has been.

The Renaissance was a purely mental and cultural thing. It was not meeting the need of sin. The whole world was waiting for a man to re-discover salvation, for a man to grapple with the moral problem of the human race, of the church in the world; a man who would go to the Bible and, from his own experience of sin and salvation, re-discover the secret of the Christian power to change the world and to change men in it. That man was a monk, Martin Luther. He made the most important discovery of the sixteenth century and he made this discovery public and swept thousands of people into the truth of Jesus Christ. It is the most dramatic thing. The Renaissance was mental but the Reformation was moral. It tackled the real problem, which is not our lack of knowledge, it is not our lack of science, it is not our lack of music, or of art and culture, helpful though those things are. The real thing man needed to discover was that we lacked Jesus Christ and the gospel of salvation.

5

THE REFORMATION

On 31st October, 1517 Martin Luther nailed his 95 propositions, or *theses*, for discussion on the church door in Wittenberg – a door that was used as a notice board to challenge public debate. That is usually considered the date of the beginning of the Reformation. Some people now think it was November 1st. It was either that hallowed evening of Halloween (the day before All Saints' Day), or it was All Saints' Day itself. But somewhere during that week it happened. A date which I think is even more important is 15th June, 1520, when Martin Luther had a bonfire, and on that bonfire he put three things: a parchment on which was the Pope's signature, excommunicating him from the church; a book, entitled *Canon Law*, which was the book by which he was supposed to live as a monk and as a priest; and a document which he now knew to be forged, a document expressing the claims of the Papacy to represent Christ on earth.

Now that bonfire was even more significant than the nailing of the paper on the church door for this reason. In the intervening three years, Martin Luther had come to ask the right question, which he had not asked when he nailed that paper up – on the earlier occasion he was attacking not the *system* but its *abuse*. But by 1520 he was having a bonfire of the system.

Let me put it this way. Imagine that at least some people in a country are getting a little dissatisfied with the government of that country. Now they must ask, 'Is that due to the personalities running the government, or is it due to the system of government?' Which is wrong? That is the big question. This must be asked in the church, as well as in politics.

When Martin Luther nailed up his theses, he assumed that the system was all right, and one of his theses said this: 'If the Pope knew how the sellers of indulgences flayed his flock, he would rather St Peter's church was burned to ashes than be built up from the skin and bones of his sheep!' The poor man was rapidly disillusioned by the Pope himself, who when he learned that the money coming in from Germany had dropped to about a third of its former amount, excommunicated this man for causing such a drop in the finance. The Pope would rather have St Peter's built on the skin and bones and Luther was wrong. This made him ask: is it the *system* that is wrong? He came to the conclusion that it was. So Luther had a bonfire in

1520, which really was the break. Before that he was trying to spring-clean the church. Three years later he began to demolish it. Before that he thought all that was needed was reform. Now he saw that very much more than that was needed.

Now I want to ask: is the Reformation a dead issue? Is it out of date? I have prayed for holy boldness in tackling this question fairly and frankly. Let me begin by being frank. I once attended a meeting of local Protestant ministers and members. And 'muggins' who is always opening his mouth and putting his foot in it, mentioned the Reformation, and was informed in no uncertain terms that this was more than a gaffe in such a situation. Protestants do not care now for the Reformation. It is a bit of dead history, and it is not the 'done thing' to bring it up in Protestant circles. I came away with a flea in my ear for having dared to mention the Reformation among Protestants.

But it was my privilege to go and visit a Roman Catholic seminary for training priests in Arklow, in the South east corner of Ireland, and speak to the tutors and lecturers of that college about (among other things) the Reformation. They wanted to hear what I thought about it, and to discuss it in an open forum. I said, 'I think the issues that were raised then are still alive, and that they have not been settled yet.'

They said, 'That's exactly what we think too.'

We had a most friendly discussion, and finished with a nice tea and I came home, after three hours talking together. It is an extraordinary position when I can talk about the Reformation to Roman Catholics, but I can't talk about it to Protestants! That is a hint as to the ultimate answer I want to give to this question: is the Reformation a dead bit of history? Is it out of date? My answer in a nutshell is that it is not out of date! But since we are not fighting people but principles we must identify where the battle line is, and the front line is now very differently drawn from the days in which Martin Luther lived.

Now let me say that during those three years, Martin Luther was a man who had come to get his priorities right. And there are seven priorities that he got right, seven things that he had in second place that he put into first place. I believe every Christian today needs to get these priorities right, just as much as he did.

1. HE PUT *CONSCIENCE* BEFORE *AUTHORITY*

The world has always been changed and led by men who put conscience before authority. The world is not led by jellyfish who have no backbone and drift with the tide. The world is ever led by people who have the courage of their convictions and who, when a thing is wrong, dare to say so, and to say so clearly, fairly and lovingly. Martin Luther was such a person.

Now it is difficult for us who live in a society where freedom of conscience is taken for granted, to realise what it is like to live in a country where it is not, where you are not able to believe what your conscience tells you and to hold the religion that your conscience tells you. Yet perhaps half the world is living under those conditions, in what we call a totalitarian state, in which the state claims a total control over people, their minds as well as their bodies. In twentieth century Britain we tended to take the right of free speech for granted, but what we need to remember is that Martin Luther was brought up in a world in which people were not allowed to think as freely as their conscience would dictate.

It was beginning to crack open. But if you want to know the kind of world in which he was brought up, study the tragic story of Galileo who, through his telescope, discovered things about the universe. The church said, 'You must not believe that! And you must not teach that. We will tell you what is true about the universe.' It was not a world in which the state said this; it was a world in which the church said: this is what you believe; this is how you behave. Martin Luther stands as a giant of a man, because he was one of those who said: my conscience I put above all the authority that is brought to bear upon me. 'Here I stand, I can do no other. So help me God, Amen!' But what preceded those words? He said, 'It is neither safe nor honest to go against one's conscience!' Here was a man who put his conscience first, and the world still needs people who will put their conscience before every kind of social pressure. His little tract on

Christian liberty reveals more than anything else, his belief in a freedom of a person to follow his own conscience in matters of religion and belief, a freedom that is often taken for granted, but which the majority of the human race still do not enjoy.

Even nonconformists today seem to conform. We are so easily led. We are so easily put under pressure. Young people who are against the establishment – watch them, they conform to each other so easily! What we want are true nonconformists who say, 'Here I stand. I don't care what pressure is brought upon me. This is right and I will do it whatever anyone else thinks, or says or does to me. Here I stand.' Martin Luther was a man who put conscience before authority and before every other kind of pressure brought to bear upon him.

2. HE PUT *TRUTH* BEFORE *UNITY*

Conscience is a fickle thing; conscience could lead you astray unless you got this second priority right. Martin Luther was a man who put truth before unity. His conscience was not free to follow any whim or desire or capricious affection of his own heart. His conscience was captive. He said, 'My *conscience* is captive to the *Word of God*', and when he said that, he was putting truth before unity.

Do you realise, in Western Europe, for well nigh 1,000 years there had only been *one* major denomination, one church? And one of the charges made against Martin Luther, and made frequently, in the last ten years, has been this: he was guilty of the crime of splitting the church; he was a schismatic – and one of the worst things he ever did was that he divided the church of Jesus Christ. People are saying this today more than they have ever done. I want to praise Martin Luther for putting truth before unity and for saying there is one thing even more important than holding a church together, and it is *truth*. He realised that what saves men and women is not the unity of the church but the truth of the gospel. Even if you unite all the churches tomorrow, that will not increase the number of people who get saved. What is really needed is the truth of the gospel being preached in those churches. In other words, truth comes before unity.

Now may I say that we are desperately in need of this today, for the one catchword is *unity*! The bandwagon – on which, if you don't climb, you will be extremely unpopular – is unity. This is the cry of a world which is shrinking because of its transport and expansion in population. We know now that we have got to learn to live together. Politically, commercially and in other ways, *unity* is the cry of our era. And the church seems to have picked up the echo of this cry and is crying: 'Unity, unity, unity!'

I want to say, very forcefully, that our day is crying out for men and women who will put truth before unity and say, 'We will have unity on *one* basis, and that is the truth of the gospel.' Given that, we want as much unity as possible, but not given that, we are not interested in unity. That was Martin Luther's position. They said, 'Look, you are going to split a church that has been one for a thousand years. Don't you feel this? Recant, and leave the church intact. If you go on like this you will break it.' But Martin Luther said he was captive to the Word of God and that truth came first. The truth of the gospel was even more important than the unity of the church. To my mind that is what is needed today, some five hundred years later, when there is a tremendous cry for unity, I believe, at the expense of truth. What is truth? Well that comes to our third priority. Where do you find the truth? How do you know that he has it, or you have it or the other person has it? Where is this truth on which we can build our unity?

3. HE PUT *SCRIPTURE* BEFORE *TRADITION*

It may surprise you to know that Martin Luther was twenty years old before he got a Bible to read for himself, although he was brought up a devout church member and he was prepared for a holy life. When he read it, he discovered to his astonishment that much of what he had been told was a vital part of Christian belief and behaviour, was not to be found in that book. He searched it through and through, and he thought, 'There is nothing here about praying to Mary. There is nothing here about praying to saints. There is nothing here about relics and images. There is nothing here about purgatory. There is nothing here about penance.' So he went on and he began to ask, 'Where did all these other things come from?' He was told the official answer: 'These are the traditions of the church which are as much the Word of God as that Book.'

He was faced with a dilemma here. He was faced with two 'words' of God – one written and the other spoken, one scripture and the other called tradition. He was told, 'Both are the truth and you must accept both.' But Martin Luther came through to the position where he said, 'That is the truth and every tradition of every church there has ever been must be brought to the touchstone of this truth and tested by it' – and, when he did that, he began to throw out tradition.

We are all creatures of tradition. Our churches have their own traditions. We have unscriptural traditions in our churches. Every church develops its tradition which is faithfully passed on to the new members, assuming that it has got the same sanction as everything else we do and say in the church. But it has not. And the traditions of a given church must always be put under the Word of God, scripture before tradition. We desperately need this today because I do believe we need changes in our churches and the changes are to be governed by this: What does the Word of God say about it? That is the constitution of every church that dares to name itself after Christ. It is by scripture that we test all our tradition.

I met a man named Edoardo Labanchi.[1] He is a man who had been Lecturer in New Testament

Theology in a college in Rome which trained the 'cream' of the priests of Rome: the Jesuits. That man had been a Roman missionary in Sri Lanka, where he had slipped into a Pentecostal church which had made him begin to think. He came back to Rome and taught the New Testament. But there came a time when, by studying the scriptures, just as Martin Luther (who was also a Professor of Theology) did centuries earlier, he came to the conclusion that he could no longer teach students that things were the word of God and the very truth when they were not in this book. That man taught himself *out* of that job. He went on to train evangelists in Rome to go out all over Italy. It was this book that had done it and he had come to the same position: scripture before tradition. Every tradition we have must be tested by the truth of God's holy word. We need men who get that priority right.

The British Council of Churches in Nottingham once said, 'We can sort this question out from within a united church.' I was thrilled when the Baptist Union, alone among the denominations of England, wrote back and said, 'No, we must sort it out first and then unite.' That is putting truth before unity and that is putting scripture before tradition. We will never get anywhere if we are trying to unite traditions. They are too different. They are too mixed. When we say 'scripture first' and our traditions very much second, then I think we shall get somewhere.

4. HE PUT *FAITH* BEFORE *WORKS*

The biggest question you can ever ask is this: how do I get right with God? How do I get forgiveness of my sins? If you have never been troubled about the question of how you get forgiveness, however do you hope to face God? Martin Luther nearly lost his life in a thunderstorm and it made him afraid to die. It made him afraid to face God because he had not got his sins forgiven. He tried desperately to find his way through to that. It was a real issue to Martin Luther and it is a real issue to everyone, for we have all got to die and after that is the Judgment.

How do you get forgiveness? When John Tetzel came round selling it in indulgences, Martin Luther was quite sure that was not the way. He said that you cannot buy forgiveness. But then he went on and took another step and realised this: If you can't buy forgiveness, you cannot earn it either.

I don't think a Christian would ever dream of saying that you can buy, with money, forgiveness from God. But I wonder how many still think they can earn it! I know there are hundreds of people in many communities who think they can. They have told me. They say, 'Well, I have never done anybody any harm and I've tried to do some good.' And if you ask, 'Why do you say that?' it is because they hope they have earned their way to heaven. Now if you would ask the world how you get saved and get to heaven they will say 'You do good deeds.' If you had asked the church of Martin Luther's day, they would have said, 'No, that's not enough. You need two things. You need to believe and you need to do good deeds.' If you had asked Martin Luther the question, he would have said, 'No, only one thing: you need to believe.'

There were the three answers. All religion comes under one of those three heads and Christianity comes under the third – 'Believe in the Lord Jesus and you will be saved'. Martin Luther got that priority right – *faith*. You are not saved by a mixture of faith and good deeds and you are certainly not saved by good deeds, because frankly, there is not a person in the world who can ever do enough good deeds!

But the manifesto of the Reformation which came out of the Old Testament into the New and from there into Martin Luther was this: 'the just shall live by faith'. That is the manifesto – not by good deeds, not by faith and good deeds, but by faith, full stop. And this Latin tag *sola fide* which means *faith alone* became the great banner of the Reformation. Faith alone – a person believes and goes to heaven.

At this point someone will say, 'Well, surely good deeds have something to do with the Christian life?' Yes, they have, and Martin Luther realised that and this is how he put it (I don't think it could be put better): 'We are saved, not *by* good deeds but *for* good deeds.' There it is in a nutshell. You don't do good deeds in order to get to heaven, you do good deeds because you are going to heaven. And that is a completely different way of thinking.

So Martin Luther had his place for good deeds, but it was not to earn forgiveness, it was not to get to heaven, it was to express the faith that had opened the kingdom of heaven, as it does, to all believers. So he got this priority right: faith before works.

Has that issue become dead? Far from it! You stop anybody in the street and ask, 'Do you hope to go to heaven – if there is a heaven? How do you hope to get there?' You will find this is as live an issue as it was then. You will find the world's answer is, 'Do good deeds. Be kind to your neighbour. Help those who suffer.' Our Lord told us to do that, but he didn't say, 'That is how you earn your forgiveness.' He didn't say, 'That's how you get to heaven.' The tragedy is that in our day, as in Luther's day, there are preachers in churches who are saying that it is a mixture of faith plus works. One of the last publications from our now defunct Baptist Press was a theologian's book saying just that – that if we could agree with that we could re-unite with Rome, that we are saved by faith plus works. But we are justified by faith and have peace with God. Martin Luther got his priorities right. We are not saved *by* good deeds; we are saved *for* good deeds.

5. HE PUT *GRACE* BEFORE THE *SACRAMENTS*

Luther was brought up to believe that there were seven sacraments. (There had been fourteen.) He was told that everybody needs the grace of God and that if you want that, the grace of God has been parcelled up in the sacraments and if you take the sacraments you get the grace. The view had come to be held that a sacrament works automatically, regardless of who administers it and who receives it, because the grace of God is in it. So there was a 'magical' view that baptism, performed on a baby who didn't know a thing about it, by a priest of mixed character, saved that baby from damnation.

Furthermore, it was believed that bread and wine, when used in Christian worship, changed at a certain point in the service and became the body and actual blood of Jesus which were then offered as a sacrifice, not on a table, but on an altar by a priest to God. You were not allowed to take the cup, and if you got the wafer, then automatically the grace of God came into your life.

Martin Luther thought that through and decided he could not believe it. He knew the grace of God was needed, but found nothing in the Bible to indicate that grace is wrapped up in sacraments which operate automatically. He began to realise that without faith the sacraments are no use – that without faith there is no grace, that 'by grace are you saved through faith' – not through sacraments, but through faith.

Is that emphasis and priority needed today? I

believe that one thing that keeps thousands of our fellow countrymen away from Christ is that they honestly believe their christening saved them and made them a Christian. Such superstitious and magical views as were held of the sacraments in the Middle Ages are not yet dead. I have met women who would not go out shopping until they had their baby 'done'. May I say this: If you do not come with faith to the communion table there is no grace for you in the bread and wine. Indeed, there could be worse than 'no grace at all', there could be judgment for you. Grace is not parcelled up in sacraments. Grace is flowing like a river. It flows free, and the simplest believer who has never been baptised and has not had the Lord's Supper knows the grace of God. Otherwise I would have to believe that hundreds of my friends in the Salvation Army know nothing of the grace of God, because they have no sacraments. But I know they have grace. They are always singing about it and they are thrilled to know that they have the grace of God. Grace is not parcelled up in the sacraments but to those who believe in God, then the sacraments come in.

Only two of them did the Lord Jesus give you – baptism and the Lord's Supper – said Martin Luther. Mind you, to be quite fair, Luther never thought this right through to its logical conclusion and he got a little mixed up over both baptism and the Lord's Supper, as his closest friends would have to admit. What he did, though, was to get the priority right: Grace before sacraments. Find the grace of God and the sacraments mean something.

6. HE PUT THE *PEOPLE* BEFORE THE *PRIESTS*

Luther was born into a church of a particular character, a pyramid: at the bottom were the people, and the top part (they were divided very rigidly) was composed of priests. There was a hierarchy, a pyramid of power, within that. The Pope was at the top of the pyramid. Then you had the Cardinals, bishops, the various orders of monks and it went right down to the parish priest.

Even the church buildings in which they worshipped were divided, and at one end was the priest and everybody at the other end was people. At one end Roman togas, now called surplices, were worn and everyone at the other end wore ordinary dress. There was this clear division right through the church: Clergy – Laity; Priests – People.

As you looked at the priests you saw this pyramid of power, heading up higher and higher. Martin Luther looked at it all and said, 'I am going to begin at the top. What justification is there for one man at the top like that? None.' He came down a bit and said, 'What justification is there for bishops?' He said, 'None.' He came down further and he said, 'Priests. What justification is there for priests in the scripture?' And his answer was 'None'. He finally came to the most incredible but wonderful re-discovery in what he called the *priesthood of all believers*. He made all the people priests and all the priests people. He saw that, in fact, there was absolutely no division between them. He saw that there were differences of function in the church, but he considered these differences of function as only that and no more, as the different functions of people are like organs within the body, and so he called them ministers – those who minister to the body. But every believer is a priest. To say that there was no priesthood within the Christian church but only people who are priests was revolutionary. This is why, though at the beginning of his life as a Roman Catholic professor of theology he taught the Bible in Latin to priests, three years later he was translating that book into common, vulgar German to give it to the people.

Luther was a man of the people by heredity, by environment (his father was a poor miner). But Luther was above all a man of the people by Christian conviction. He said, 'It is the people who should have the Bible, not the priests.' So he said, 'I am going to give this Bible in the German language to the people in such a way that a maid, sweeping a room with a broom, knows more of this than the priests.' He did that, giving them the Bible in their own language. He was seeking to help the people to be priests, and that is a re-discovery of a New Testament position in which there are no priests except every believer.

Is that protest out of date? Two-thirds of the professing Christians of the world still live under priesthood and under hierarchical control. The protest is still desperately needed. Let us break down this division between clergy and laity, priest and people. It is not a scriptural one. We are *all* ministers; we are *all* members; we are *all* priests; we are *all* the people. And the word *laity* means *people of God*. We are *all* the laity and we are *all* the priesthood and we are *all* in Christ. Luther thought in terms of a church that is composed entirely of people, entirely of priests, with no division and no pyramid of power. I would say again that that is desperately needed today.

7. HE PUT *CHRIST* BEFORE THE *CHURCH*, THE *HEAD* BEFORE THE *BODY*

This was the big crunch, the big question. I remember one Saturday afternoon, my tutor in Church History said, 'What do *you* think was the biggest issue in the Reformation?' I told him this and he agreed: 'It was that Martin Luther challenged the idea that Christ and the church were one.' He challenged the idea that the church could do for people what Christ can do for them. He challenged the very notion that the church is Christ and that the body now fulfils the functions of the head. Now let me explain what I mean.

'I need a prophet to tell me infallibly the word and the truth of God. Who is my prophet? The head or the body?' Martin Luther said, 'The head is my infallible teacher,' and the Romans said, 'No, the body is the infallible teacher.' And it is this that, more than anything, still divides us: the belief in an infallible church.

I need a *priest* to come to God. Who is my priest? The Reformers said, 'Jesus Christ, the head, is my priest and I need no other to come to God.' And we still believe that and you can come to God at any time through Jesus Christ. If you have got sins to confess, go to your priest in heaven and confess them. But the Romans said, 'The church which is his body is my priest and I must confess my sin to the body.'

I need a king to reign over me and tell me what to do and control my behaviour. Who is my king? The answer of the Protestant is, 'The king is my head in heaven.' The answer of the Roman is, 'The body of Christ on earth is king and must reign.'

This is the big difference. Martin Luther saw straight through this and he dared to call the papacy Antichrist. Now let us just realise what he meant by that, because what he said was absolutely true. He did not mean that the Pope was *against* Jesus. He was not. The word *anti* doesn't mean *against*. It does now in modern English, but it didn't then. And it doesn't in the New Testament. It means *instead of*. Anyone who puts himself instead of Christ is *anti Christ*. Martin Luther accused the Roman church of being Antichrist on this ground. He said, 'It is Christ to whom we must go and you have said, "You must come through us". You are putting yourself in the place of Christ. The body is replacing the head.'

At this point they came back on him with a very important statement. They said, 'Ah! But when the head is in heaven and somebody on earth wants to come, haven't they got to come through the body? And therefore is not the head of the body on earth (listen carefully!) – Christ's vicar?' The word *vicar* means *someone who is in the place of another*. *Vicarious* – means *to be a replacement for someone else*. 'Surely,' they said, 'Christ has got to convey from heaven to earth his teaching. How does he do it? Through his vicar who is the papal successor in Rome.' Martin Luther thought that one through and he came to this scriptural conclusion. Yes, Christ must have a vicar on earth to speak for him and that vicar is the Holy Ghost. The Holy Ghost speaks to people on Christ's behalf.

May I sum up this point by saying this: Martin Luther was virtually saying, and anybody who accepts the New Testament must say, 'I will have no priest but Christ and no vicar but the Holy Ghost.' That is the Reformation priority. Christ the head is the one who saves. If you want forgiveness of sins, I can't give it to you. Neither can any church. You must go to Jesus Christ, the priest to whom we went. And you must go because the same Holy Spirit, who has spoken to us, spoke to you.

Is that protest a bit of dead history or is it still needed today? Is the battle over? No. Then where is the front line drawn? I say with all honesty now and with pain in my heart that the front line is no longer between Protestants and Roman Catholics.

That is why those who only fire in one direction are out of date. The tragedy is that scores and scores of Protestants have got their priorities wrong over the last hundred years and the battle is now between evangelicals on the one hand and many Protestants and Roman Catholics on the other. I am giving you there the considered judgment of a French professor who published a book *The Heirs of the Reformation* in which he writes, 'Who are the true heirs of Martin Luther? The Protestants of today? No. But the evangelicals who put scripture above everything else and who put Jesus Christ above everyone else.' That is where the battle is being fought and it is going to be a very difficult battle. He calls for men and women who will still say, 'Here I stand. I can do no other.'

But may I say two things in closing. First, we are not fighting people. I am not against Roman Catholics and I am not against Protestants. I am against 'isms'. I am against systems. I want to love people whoever they are, as people wanted by the Lord, as people who want to have the truth as it is in Christ Jesus. I found a love in my heart for them, but I hate the systems that blind people to the truth and I pray for a righteous indignation that is as courageous in this day as Martin Luther was in his.

The other thing I want to say is this, for I am sure you are asking it: Why fight, in a day when people want to be together? Why argue about these things? Surely it is doctrinal quibbling. Why not all come together? After all, we worship the same God. Why go on fighting in a day when people want tolerance more than truth, in a day when everybody is so friendly and comes together? Isn't this obscurantism, isn't it going back to the Dark Ages? Why fight? Because *this* is the truth of God and no other, that is why. Because the salvation of souls is at stake, that is why. If you tell a man that baptism saves him, you damn him. If you tell a man that if he does good works he will get to heaven you are sending him straight to hell. And because nice though it would be to get together on earth with any and every and no view of God, it is in the next world we have got to live for eternity and it is the God of Jesus Christ we have got to meet and it is this God who sent Jesus Christ for a sacrifice for sins to be the *only* priest we need to bring us at last to heaven, saved by his precious blood. It is that Jesus that we preach. The salvation of immortal souls is at stake. Is that worth fighting for? Or would you rather have it on your conscience that, for the sake of peace, you allowed people to say and to do and to think things that caused hundreds to go the wrong way into a lost eternity. That is the issue.

Praise God for Martin Luther, for his honesty, for his courage to stand alone for what he knew was right and true; and pray to God that he will yet raise up more men who, in love, will declare the truth and say, 'Here I stand. I can do no other.' To go against conscience is neither safe nor honest. My conscience is captive to the Word of God and therefore I put conscience before authority. I put truth before unity. I put scripture before tradition and I put faith before works and I put grace before sacraments and I put people before priests – and indeed believers are priests – and I put Christ before the church and anything and everyone else.

That is ultimately the issue. Martin Luther upheld Christ and got people's eyes away from everyone else because, at the beginning of his experience, he had had his eyes on too many people. He had prayed to saints, three every day, twenty-one different saints a week. He had prayed to Mary. He had gone on pilgrimages and looked at relics and images. Then he saw that none of this had brought him assurance of forgiveness of his sins. Later, he was talking to his saintly superior, Von Staupitz, who said to him, 'Martin Luther, if you take away all these things that you call crutches to a tottering faith, if you take away Mary, if you take away the saints, if you take away images, if you take away penance and pilgrimages, if you take away all this, what will you put in their place?' Do you remember the answer of Martin Luther? –'Jesus Christ.' Man only needs Jesus Christ, and when we say that, and say it clearly, then people will be saved, for they look at him.

[1] Edoardo Labanchi – read his testimony in the book *Far from Rome, near to God* (Banner of Truth).

6

REFORMERS, ROMAN CATHOLICS AND RADICALS

The Reformation which Martin Luther started became a revolution because more and more was changed and different people began to change it.

There are three groups of people we need to look at. First of all, the Reformers. We began by considering Martin Luther, but there were others. Secondly, we need to ask what the Roman Catholics were doing all this time. How did they react to what was happening in Germany? Thirdly, I want to look at a group that has been called the radicals.

THE REFORMERS

We will look at the Reformers in three different countries: Germany, Switzerland and England, and ask of each country how much was changed there and who changed it.

THE REFORMATION IN GERMANY

Who changed things? As we have seen, Martin Luther did. How much did he change? The answer is that during the first four or five years of Martin Luther's epoch-making discoveries he changed a great deal. He got rid of the Pope, bishops, indulgences and the doctrine of purgatory. He got rid of a host of things and reduced the sacraments from seven to two.

Then came the crisis during which he had to go into hiding in the Wartburg Castle. When he came out of hiding he found to his horror that some of his friends were carrying the change much further than he intended and much more quickly. The truth is that at a certain point Martin Luther stopped changing things. Consequently, he kept a lot of things that Rome had. For example: he kept candles on the altar – something Rome did, but the Bible certainly doesn't have; he kept crucifixes, as you may still notice in Lutheran churches today; and he kept images and pictures. Above all, he kept his own traditional practice and relationship to the Lord's Supper and baptism, and somehow he still believed that the bread and wine actually were the body and blood of Christ. He never quite got over that. He kept the practice of infant baptism, and when people said, 'Surely faith is needed in baptism?', his reply was, 'Well, who is to say that the baby doesn't have faith?'

You can see at this point that Martin Luther, having changed a tremendous amount initially, put the brakes on and stopped changing, and the Lutheran church has, by and large, to this day, stopped at that point where he stopped. Therefore there are still many things that would surprise you if you went into a Lutheran church building, given that we count Lutherans among the Protestants.

Now the other question, 'How much did he change?' I have already tried to answer.

But 'Who changed it?' Here we come to rather a startling answer. Luther got the princes to change things. In other words, this was a state change.

Lutheranism, like Romanism was an established religion and from the very beginning Luther relied on the princes, the dukes and the Elector of Saxony, in particular, a man called Frederick; he relied on them to reform from the top. Those who ruled the land also were regarded by Luther as ruling the church. The upshot of this was that at a famous Diet (council) at Speyer, it was decided that each area would adopt the religion of its prince. If you lived in an area where the prince was Roman Catholic, you were a Roman Catholic.

Can you see the weakness in this? Can you see the point at which the Reformation stopped in Germany? First, it stopped at the point that not everything was changed; then it stopped at the point where, instead of allowing others to be as free with their conscience as Martin Luther was, they decided that certain areas of Germany would be Protestant and certain areas would be Roman Catholic.

Funnily enough, a group of people objected

violently to that and they made a protest against that division, and that was the origin of the word 'Protestant'. It was those who *protested* against splitting up and saying, 'Everybody *here* will be *this* religion and everybody *there* will be *that*.'

It was the state that was settling the issue of religion and the obvious result came in the beginning of the seventeenth century when the Roman Catholic states got together and went to war with the Protestants, who also got together, and the Thirty Years' war took place. That is the kind of 'end product' of this kind of mistake. Sooner or later you will have religious wars.

So much for Germany. That pattern spread from Germany to Denmark, Sweden and Norway. All these countries adopted Lutheranism as a state religion, adopted for every citizen within the country.

THE REFORMATION IN SWITZERLAND
Martin Luther didn't start the Reformation in Switzerland, nor did he help it. It began on its own and there were two men who were at the heart of it. One was German Swiss and the other French. The German Swiss was Ulrich Zwingli, an ordinary parish priest for the Roman Catholic church in a small country village in the German part of Switzerland. He became a Protestant by reading his Greek New Testament. Exactly the same thing happened to him as would happen to Martin Luther. Reading his New Testament, Zwingli realised that

many of the things he was teaching from his pulpit weren't true. The interesting thing is that Zwingli was invited to be the priest at the Cathedral of Zurich. If ever you are in Zurich go and look at the cathedral. Zwingli got up and he preached, and he preached the new truth he had found in this book. He swept Zurich with him. Among other things he said it was wrong for the Pope to have an army, and to staff the army with Swiss mercenary troops. If you go to the Vatican today you will see the Swiss troops guarding the Vatican to this very day, and Zwingli was speaking against that, but of course he spoke against many other things. He finally left his allegiance to the Pope and got married. These two things often seem to go together. Many priests followed him.

He finally persuaded the City Council (notice that) to say that everybody in Zurich must now be a Protestant. Once again the same dreadful mistake was made, but they carried it through and they became officially Protestant.

All the valleys leading from Zurich became Protestant. The trouble was that people in the mountains and the forests didn't and very soon the valley people and the mountain people fought. The war, which lasted two years, was fought in the Zurich district, and during that war Zwingli himself who was fighting, was slain at a little place called Kappel.

Once again, the same pattern: going to the state, going to the secular authority to impose your religious views on a district, leads to war.

Before he died, Zwingli had a big argument with Luther over the Lord's Supper. Luther's position was that the bread *is* the body, and that wine *is* the blood of Jesus, and Zwingli said: that is just bread, and that is just wine – symbols of his body and blood. I'm afraid that is why the Germans and the Swiss never got together in the Reformation.

Now the story moves to France and a young man called John Calvin, born in Picardy, the son of a lawyer. His father put him into the Law and he went to Paris, Orleans and Bourges universities to study it. That is where Calvin got his logical mind. He remained a lawyer to his dying day, in his speech, his clarity of thinking and his devastating arguments. It is Calvin's arguments that persuaded a lot of people to be what are called 'Calvinists'. He went to Paris, studied the Greek New Testament, and was converted in 1532.

How many Christians today have studied the Greek New Testament? I met an ordinary member of a church who spends all his days working with his hands and yet who taught himself Greek so that he could read the New Testament in its original language. There was one church, started in the last century where you couldn't be a member unless you could read the Greek New Testament. That is interesting, isn't it? I commend it to you. It converted Luther. It converted Zwingli and now it converted this man, John Calvin.

Within months he was in prison for his Christian

views – in Paris. Finally, let out of prison, he fled as a refugee and he spent the days travelling around. He found himself in the Swiss city of Basel at the age of 26, and he decided to write down his Christian beliefs: *The Institutes of the Christian Religion*, some 600 pages in each volume, and still acclaimed as one of the greatest expositions of Protestant faith in the whole world. Mind you, there are some things in it that will raise your eyebrows, such as his views on Sunday: he advocated going to church on Sunday morning and playing bowls on Sunday afternoon. He did that himself, and it is to John Calvin that we owe the 'Continental Sunday' as it has been called. That is an interesting little side-light on Calvin for you! But he said many things that are much more important and much deeper.

Above all, Calvin believed that God was on the throne. He believed in the sovereignty of God and that God's will is the final factor that decides the history of nations and of men, and it is because of that tremendous logical emphasis on divine sovereignty and the doctrine of predestination that Calvin gave his name to people who think that way, as Calvinists. Calvin believed in that, and so did Martin Luther, so did Zwingli and so did all the reformers – that God is on the throne and that God is in absolute control of everything and everyone. It is a mighty work for a young man of 26 to write, and that writing has influenced the course of history.

John Calvin was still fleeing from one place

to another as a refugee and one day, trying to get back into France, he discovered that a minor war was going on right in this road, so he took a detour and failed to get to his destination by the evening, so he settled down in the place where he was for the night. The place was Geneva and having taken that detour, he went on to stay for twenty years, and Geneva became the centre of Presbyterianism for the whole world. It is the most incredible story. Word got around that John Calvin, the young author of these books, was in Geneva and the local parish priest, a fine man called William Farel, hastened round to the Inn and said, 'Calvin, I want you to stay here.' He said, 'A year ago, the council decided that Geneva should be Protestant.' Notice that again, by the way. He said, 'It just hasn't worked out. They are getting as drunk as ever, they are gambling as much as ever. Nothing has happened. The people aren't changing so we need a man like you, John Calvin. We need you – stay here', and he pleaded with him. John Calvin said, 'Alright, I will stay.'

So John Calvin became the Reformer of Geneva. Mind you, he was pretty strict. He wasn't having funny goings on. He would haul a man up before the church and pass him to the magistrates for doing this, that and the other, but he pulled that city round until it became a well-behaved city. I say 'city', but we must have the right idea of the size of towns in those days – 13,000 in Geneva – but with strict discipline he cleaned up the city and he became so unpopular that three years later he had to run for his life. He fled to Strasbourg, but after he departed the city collapsed and things went from bad to worse so they sent a deputation from the city council: 'Please come back', and back came John Calvin.

He worked out a further Reformation. He went much, much further in the changes. For example, he wouldn't have crucifixes, he wouldn't have candles, and (dare I say it?) he wouldn't have organs either. He said the people should sing. He carried the changes further than Martin Luther ever did. He also instituted what is now known as the Presbyterian system of church government in which the church is governed by bodies of laymen and pastors and elders together, in which those local bodies meet in representative assemblies and look after wider areas of churches.

Geneva became a place to which Protestants fled for refuge, and altogether 6000 more came to live there who were running away from persecution, and, of course, they picked up Calvin's ideas. When it was safe for them to return to their own countries, they took with them Calvin's ideas of faith and his ideas of how to run the church, but once again Calvin made the mistake of putting the church and state together, only this time he didn't say the state must govern the church, but the church must govern the state. It didn't lead to war in Geneva though it did elsewhere.

From Geneva, France was influenced and the Protestants there were more like Calvin than Luther in Germany. They became known as Huguenots and their numbers grew dramatically. If you know your history you will recall that on one terrible St Bartholomew's Day, August 24th, 1572, 22,000 French Huguenots were slaughtered, 2000 of them in Paris alone. They were put to death throughout France and the survivors fled, many to England and the Netherlands.

THE REFORMATION IN SCOTLAND

The country most heavily influenced by Geneva was Scotland. Four great Scotsmen must be mentioned in connection with the Reformation. Patrick Hamilton started the Reformation north of the border. He was burned in 1528 but his work was taken over by George Wishart, who had been to Switzerland. But he likewise came to a sticky end fairly quickly. But the man who really did it finally was John Knox. A most colourful character, he studied at Glasgow University and went to be Chaplain of St.Andrew's castle, for the Scottish army. The French took the castle, took John Knox away as a prisoner and sold him as a galley slave. There he was, rowing the galleys, but the English rescued him, he came to England, and then got into trouble with Queen Mary and fled to the continent and to Geneva – to John Calvin.

Knox was a young man just ripe for all these views, and he came back to his native Scotland, saying, 'Lord, give me Scotland, or I die.' The Lord gave him Scotland and John Knox began his work. Alas, in 1559 he persuaded the Scottish Parliament to become Protestant. In 1560 they had their first General Assembly, but in 1561 the beautiful and wily Mary, Queen of Scots came back, and with her beauty and her wile she got round most of the Protestant nobles in Scotland – and there they were, Mary, Queen of Scots and John Knox face to face. It is a most dramatic story and if you have a sense of history, you must read it.

Nevertheless, after a civil war in which Mary Queen of Scots was captured, and abdicated in favour of her infant boy James, and ultimately was beheaded for treason by Elizabeth I of England, John Knox's teaching won ground and Scotland became Presbyterian.

The Church of Scotland reflects the church of Geneva while the Church of England is much nearer to Lutheran churches. The Church of Scotland owed everything to John Knox. When he died, the leadership was taken by the last great Scot I want to mention, Andrew Melville, who said to King James, 'Sire, there are two kings and two kingdoms in Scotland. There is King James, of whom I am a loyal subject, and there is the Lord Jesus Christ of whom James is a subject, and all who are in his church'.

THE REFORMATION IN ENGLAND

The English Reformation was a typical English compromise. We muddle through and say, 'Oh, that will do.' We don't work by principles, we are terribly pragmatic, saying 'Does it work?' and

'Whatever works is right.'

It started, of course, with Henry VIII and the fact that he wanted to marry another woman. Mind you, that has been greatly misinterpreted and misunderstood. Let me give you the facts: Henry VIII was forced by others to marry Catherine of Aragon and it was an illegal marriage because she was his brother's widow. Therefore he should never have married her, but under pressure from others, including the Pope, who gave him special permission to marry illegally, he was pressed into this marriage for political reasons. Every child she had was stillborn, except one – the little girl Mary who was later to become the infamous Bloody Mary. He had no son to carry on the Tudor line and he knew that when he was dead, civil war would break out unless there was a son. Most people in England took it as a sign that God's judgment was on this marriage, and that it wasn't a legal marriage and he should never have entered into it – for God had not given him a son. That is the background.

Then he met Anne Boleyn with whom he really fell in love and who would have made a good Queen and who would have been a legal wife. Do you see the tangle? I am not justifying Henry VIII, simply giving you the facts. He applied to the Pope for an annulment of his first (illegal) marriage, but by now politics had changed and the Pope, for political reasons, said, 'No, you can't have a special divorce, or a special annulment on the grounds of illegally marrying this woman.' So

Henry VIII said, 'All right. From now on I don't obey the Pope.' With one step after another, Henry separated the English church from the Pope as England is separated by the English Channel from the continent. For example, he made himself 'head of the church'. This was an amazing step when you consider that Henry VIII was a bit of a theologian. In his youth he had written a book against Martin Luther, and the Pope was so thrilled with the book which defended the seven sacraments of Rome that he gave him a title 'Defender of the Faith' – a title which to this day our Queen possesses, and which is on the coins in your pocket.

Henry married Anne Boleyn, mainly because he put a friend of his, Thomas Cranmer, into the Archbishopric of Canterbury. Cranmer said, 'I will annul your first marriage because I am convinced it is illegal in the first place, so I annul it. You can marry Anne Boleyn', and he secretly conducted the wedding. Henry had made himself head of the church, he had broken with Rome; he now needed money and so he seized the wealthy monasteries of England and sold their lands to other individuals, thus creating the middle class for the first time in England, which has affected social life ever since.

Henry did more than this but the main point I want to make is that Henry didn't want England to go Protestant. He wanted everything to carry on as normal, minus the monasteries because, of course, their loyalty to the Pope was pretty strong. He wanted the Church of England to carry on exactly as before, only instead of the Pope he would be Pope. That is basically and simply what he wanted, but he reckoned without a number of factors. He reckoned without the factor that the Bible was feverishly being translated into English by William Tyndale. This man was hounded around England and had to flee to the continent and was finally burnt at the stake, but Tyndale gave us the English Bible. During Henry's reign, one copy was put in every church in England, and for the first time people could go along and read it. Do you notice that every time it is the opportunity to read the Bible that sets people free and causes the most remarkable things. William Tyndale is the man who said that 'by the grace of God he would cause the boy who pushed the plough in England to know more of this book than the Pope himself!' That is precisely what began to happen and the Bible began to be read.

Henry reckoned, too, without such men as Thomas Cranmer who in his heart was sympathetic to Protestant ideas. He reckoned without a lot of other people.

Furthermore, there was a widespread resentment that the Pope still took money out of England – the tributes and other 'annuities' that were paid were called 'Peter's pence'. He reckoned without such men as Thomas Cromwell and Latimer.

Fearing the speed of change I am afraid Henry executed Romans and Reformers alike towards the end of his reign, and he died leaving England in a ferment; but he died leaving on the throne a boy of nine (Edward VI) who was a very serious little Christian, even at that age; a boy who was deeply influenced by Thomas Cranmer, Archbishop of Canterbury. This was a boy who was sympathetic to England making changes. During his brief reign certain things happened: First, clergy were allowed to marry; second, the Lord's Supper in the Church of England took on a Protestant character and the 'altar' was called a 'table'; third, and even more important, services were put into English instead of Latin for the first time, and a book was prepared called 'A Book of Common Prayer' – meaning, a book for everybody to use, not just the priest who knows Latin up at the front, but a book of common prayer so that the common people could pray.

That book, after its second revision, became the Book of Common Prayer (BCP). It is largely unchanged and still in use, although revised services began to appear in the twentieth century Church of England. It is a wonderful book, full of scriptural devotion.

One of the rules that was brought in under Edward VI was that every priest must preach at least four times a year! That provides a little insight into the state of the Church of England at that time.

Furthermore, they began to write down, under Cranmer, some Articles of Religion. They got to 42 but later it was cut down to 39. The articles set the Protestant tone of the Church of England.

During Edward VI's reign, refugees returned

from Europe and there came to Cambridge, my old university, a famous Professor of Theology from Strasbourg, Martin Bucer, who was teaching students the Protestant understanding of the gospel of Christ.

Then the boy king died and the throne was taken by his half-sister, daughter of a Spanish mother, Mary. Half-Spanish by blood and wholly Spanish in thought, she married Philip of Spain and spent more time out of the country than in, and she was determined to bring England back to Rome. 1,200 married clergy were put out of a job, the pendulum swung right back and the House of Lords and the House of Commons were made to kneel to Cardinal Pole, sent from Rome to accept again England back to the fold of the Papal See.

During Mary's reign, nearly 300 great Christians were put to death and she earned that dreadful nickname 'bloody Mary' – and she deserved it. As I travel around England I see traces of this. Go to Oxford and in the main street outside Balliol College there is a memorial to two men, Latimer and Ridley, burned at the stake during Mary's reign because of their Protestant faith. You may remember Latimer's words to Ridley, 'Be of good cheer, Master Ridley, and play the man. By God's grace we shall light such a torch in England this day that shall never be put out.' Next time you go to Oxford, look at that monument and think of those two people.

During Mary's reign Cranmer, Archbishop of

Canterbury, under great pressure, signed the paper recanting the changes he had made. But alas, you can't change that easily and in his heart he knew he was wrong and he soon found himself going to be burned at the stake. When the time came for him to be tied to the stake he publicly said that he had utter remorse about the recanting of his Protestant stand and he took the arm that had signed that paper and he plunged it into the flames and watched it until it had burned to a cinder. He said, 'That hand that signed such a paper has got to be burned first.' Hooper was burned at Gloucester and many another man was burned at the stake. You may have heard of the fires of Smithfield. Four bishops, one archbishop and many other leading preachers were put to death during Mary's reign.

You can imagine when Elizabeth I came to the throne everybody heaved a sigh of relief. She was, of course, in the Pope's eyes and in many other people's eyes, an illegitimate child. The Pope said that Mary, Queen of Scots, was the right heir to the throne.

Persecution ended and the refugees came flooding back to England. Now it was in the reign of Elizabeth I that the typical English muddle, which we call the Church of England, came to be. You see, Elizabeth didn't like the Scots. She didn't like John Knox. She didn't like Geneva. Elizabeth liked ornate services. She liked vestments and rituals, so she was unhappy about letting these things go. She said that the second Book of Common Prayer of Edward was much too Protestant and she got a number of changes in the Prayer book, putting it back towards the Roman position; and she stopped the practice of clergymen meeting to study the Bible, something which had been doing a power of good in the land. But she didn't like clergymen studying the Bible.

Yet she couldn't turn the clock back, as Mary had tried to, and the Elizabethan Settlement settled for a kind of half-way house. If you want to know why, within the Church of England today, you can have evangelicals and Anglo-Catholics, you must go back to Elizabeth I because leaving the thing in a half-way position and imposing it from Parliament, she laid the door wide open to this kind of mixture that has resulted. A church that can be such a mixture is due to a mixture of foundations and it was Elizabeth who laid that mixture.

The Book of Common Prayer is still largely (though not entirely) Protestant, and the 39 Articles that were finally drawn up in Elizabeth's reign are a wonderful statement of Protestant faith. Any preacher who preaches the 39 articles is a clergymen who will be preaching the gospel. Alas! Not everyone does, but it is there in the book and there is enough Protestantism there to have a thoroughly evangelical and Protestant Church of England. There is also the possibility of the other which came later.

Elizabeth died an unpopular queen, though her popularity came back when Philip II of Spain, incensed at the execution of Mary, Queen of Scots said, 'We are going to invade England by force and bring it back to the Pope.' He sent an 'Armada': 160 ships, 30,000 'marine commando' troops, and he had an army massed the other side of the English channel to cross as soon as the invasion had taken place. England was in desperate straits. She had no friends. The massed might of Europe seemed to be coming towards her. Up the channel came the Armada. Across the channel the troops were waiting, the army of Philip, and it seemed as if England was going to lose the day – but she had Sir Francis Drake. The story is told about him of how the Spanish Armada was routed by the superior seamanship of England and how it seemed that even God fought for England that day because the winds were too strong for those unwieldy galleons of Spain and so they were wrecked. They were wrecked on the shores of England, on the shores of Scotland, and to this day they are still searching for the wrecked galleons of the Spanish Armada.

Incidentally, I've got Spanish blood in me, due to the Armada, because a galleon was wrecked on the shores of northern Scotland and the sailors came ashore and they were called by the name of St Clair. They took local girls, settled down and became the clan of Sinclair. My mother is a Sinclair. Maybe that's why I get excited at times!

We have looked at the Reformers in Germany, Switzerland, Scotland and England. In none of these places did they carry the Reformation to its logical conclusion. In none of them did they get right back to the New Testament kind of church. In every place, church and state were too close to each other. Either the state ran the church or the church ran the state, but in every place there resulted a religion that was imposed upon an area. The whole area went Protestant and the whole area was supposed to change.

Now to my mind that was not the New Testament and that was the fatal error. It led in almost every case to war, and is there anything more tragic than people fighting wars over religion? Is there anything more tragic than people fighting in the name of Christ for Christianity and killing each other to do so? We know now that it is utterly wrong to do so, but where a state seeks to impose religion you are going to get this kind of thing and sooner or later this kind of trouble arises and war results.

WHAT WERE THE ROMAN CATHOLICS DOING AT THIS TIME?

By 1580, sixty years after Luther, Protestantism had spread through much of Germany to Denmark, Norway, Sweden, to a good deal of Switzerland, quite a bit of France and to England; and by 1580 Ireland was still Catholic, a good bit of France was still Catholic, Spain was still Catholic, Italy was still Catholic, Austria was still Catholic and parts of Switzerland and Germany were Catholic. The funny thing is that all that happened in sixty years and for the next three hundred years the boundaries stayed the same.

We must ask why it was that Protestantism spread so quickly in sixty years, then came to a line that stayed the same until the twentieth century. The answer lies in a movement among the Romans called the Counter-Reformation. There had been an attack on Rome which had robbed her of half of Europe, and Rome was not going to sit down under that. Three things happened which stemmed the flood and which drew the boundaries.

Now what happened? There was a Roman Catholic whose name was Ignatius Loyola. A Spanish nobleman, terribly wounded in the war, he lay with a shattered leg in hospital for some months, and during that time he had visions and he had a change of heart. He became a devout Roman Catholic and he believed that his call in life was to stop the spread of Protestantism, and to do that he would need a Roman Catholic army, but an army that would fight in a very different way from other armies. I could almost call his army the 'Salvation Army of Rome'. He went to Paris and gathered around himself a group of six noblemen and some noble ladies and he started 'The Society of Jesus', popularly known as the Jesuits. Ignatius Loyola saw their task as to keep Europe for Rome and to stop the flood of Protestantism, and quite frankly, he largely achieved it. He gathered around him hundreds of people and subjected them to the most rigorous military discipline you can imagine, which was set down in a book entitled *Spiritual Exercises*. For 25 days you absolutely drill yourself with fasting, seeking visions and many other things, and for that period you really go through it. By the end of that you are ready to be a Jesuit, a follower of Ignatius Loyola.

Furthermore, they were prepared to use fair means and foul and they said, 'Provided you keep somebody for Rome, you can use any means that you feel you should.' This is why the English word 'Jesuitry' in the dictionary means:'justifying the means by the end' and using any means to attain it. They got so bad at doing that, that ultimately a pope had to stop the Order. Nevertheless they had their good ones. One of the outstanding characters in that 'army of Rome' was a man called Francis Xavier who converted 700,000 people to Rome in India, the East Indies and Japan.

Now that was the first thing that happened in Rome – an army of dedicated, disciplined men who were determined to 'stop the rot', from their point of view.

Secondly, the Pope, realising that there were many things to be discussed, convened the Council of Trent, which met 25 times between the years 1545 and 1563. At first the Pope was thinking of inviting the Protestants to come and sit down and talk over the differences and see if they couldn't be resolved. He was persuaded by his cardinals not to invite the Protestants at all and they never came. Had they come, history might have been different.

It became a most reactionary Council. They pronounced the curse of God upon Protestant teaching and said, 'Anybody who believes that you are justified by faith alone, let anathema be upon that person' – the curse of God.

Then, in a series of statements, they said these things: There are seven sacraments, not two and they are necessary to be saved; tradition must be placed alongside the Bible as the word of God; the Apocrypha must be part of the Bible; Purgatory does exist; indulgences and the invocation of saints and images and relics is a right and pious practice; and the Pope has absolute authority.

That was the first time these things had been said by the church of Rome. May I say very frankly and lovingly and sincerely, not one of those things has changed yet. Indeed it can't if you believe the Councils cannot err – then how could these things be denied now? The Second Vatican Council later cleaned up many things and altered many things and explored many things, but not a single thing that I have just mentioned has been changed at all. Here was a Statement by Rome that had the effect of telling Roman Catholics what they really believed, enabling them to answer Protestant critics.

Thirdly, the Inquisition was revived; torture, imprisonment and death were used as instruments against Protestants. They were used to wipe out almost every Protestant in Spain and most Protestants in Italy and in other parts, like Austria. The result is that to this day Christians, as we understand them, are in a tiny minority in those lands.

The Inquisition, the Council of Trent, and Ignatius Loyola with his Catholic army of priests and laymen, Jesuits who were utterly disciplined and dedicated to stopping it, arrested the advance of Protestantism by the end of the sixteenth century. European regions that were Catholic at the end of the sixteenth century have largely stayed predominantly Catholic, while Protestant areas have stayed predominantly Protestant. Isn't that strange?

THE RADICALS

The Radicals are so called because they were the extreme left-wing of the Reformation. They have been called the 'step-children' of the Reformation and its 'left-wing'. So who were they?

They were people who began to ask the greatest fundamental question of all: 'Who should be doing the reforming? Who should be doing the changing?'

They came to this momentous conclusion which neither Roman nor Reformer had reached: it should have nothing to do with the state; church and state are two quite different bodies and should not get too close together. These Radicals believed in a free church, not an established one. They were not even happy with established Protestantism. They said that you can't make people good through the government. You cannot impose a religion, it must be freely and voluntarily accepted by people themselves. You can't say everybody in England is going to be Protestant. You can't say everybody in Spain must be Catholic. You can't use the state to promote religion. You can only use one sword and that is the sword of the Spirit which is the word of God.

So they were pacifists, refusing to take part in wars between Protestants and Catholics. They said that they were not going to fight for the gospel, and they were regarded as revolutionaries and were thought to be destroying the one thing that held society together, and that was the idea that church and state belonged to each other, so they were regarded as the most dangerous people.

Where did they start? They arose in 1522 in the city of Zurich in Switzerland, and they called themselves, significantly, 'Brethren'. The leaders were Conrad Grebel and Felix Manx. Fine Christians they were – in the very city where Zwingli was causing the council of the city to make everybody Protestant. They said, 'That is not the right way to do it. The only right way is to preach the word and when people voluntarily accept it, form them into a church.' They were fighting hard for what we now know as religious liberty. The United States is what it is today because of their fight. There was an established religion in Scotland, in England, in Germany. Everywhere you went you found that the state was deciding the religion, but in America the ideas of these Radicals took root, and there is separation of church from state.

They also said that not only should a church not be identified with a state, but the church should not be identified with the community. Therefore – and here comes the crunch, and they were the first to say this – a person should not be baptised until they believe. They turned from infant baptism to believer's baptism. They got the nickname 'twice baptisers'. Only it wasn't quite like that. They were called the Anabaptists, *'ana'* – meaning 'again', 'twice'. The Anabaptists were the left-wing of the Reformation. The Anabaptists were the Radicals. The Anabaptists were those who sought to go right back to the original days, to a church that is not identified or connected with the state, a church that is made up of believers only, which only baptises people when they are old enough to have faith in Jesus and therefore belong to the body of Christ, by faith.

Sadly, it was not only the Romans who attacked these people but the Reformers too. There came a day when Luther said to the German princes, 'You must use the sword against these Radicals.' And there came a day when John Calvin consented to the death by drowning of Felix Manx, as being an appropriate end for a Baptist. He was drowned. Zwingli, in Zurich, got the council to pass cruel laws against these people.

Now isn't it interesting? The Romans used the state and so did the Reformers, and both were prepared to use the literal sword in the name of Christ. The Radicals said, 'We will use no other sword than this – the Bible.' So the sword of the Romans and the sword of the Reformers were used against them. It is a tragic story, but we can now be free from the established church, because their influence and their ideas popped up in England in the time of Elizabeth I in a group of people called Independents.

The Independents wanted a free church, and because they couldn't find it in England they set off for America in the 'Mayflower' to settle for all time there the principle of religious liberty of the individual to follow whatever faith he feels is right. This is our heritage, and for this they fought and died.

They had some fanatics and extremists like Thomas Muntzer of Zwickau but, by and large, when you study their story (and the research was beginning in the twentieth century – only now have people really begun to learn the story of the Anabaptists), they fought and died for religious liberty but they only fought with the word. They were accused of being revolutionaries, but Jesus said, 'My kingdom is not of this world. Else would my servants fight.' That is what the Anabaptists said.

There were men like Menno Simons. If you have ever come across the Mennonites, you owe those great Christians to him. There was Jakob Hutter, and if you have ever come across the Hutterites, you owe those to him. These, to my mind, were the ultimate Reformers. It was they who said, 'We will change everything that is not according to the word of God and *we* will change it, we will not expect princes or popes to change it; we will live by and follow the word of God as individuals and fellowships.'

In the next chapter we will take this story into the seventeenth century, the age when religious liberty came to England, when people began to be allowed to follow their own convictions, the age of William Penn, John Bunyan, and many other great servants of God. Let us thank God that there were those who carried the Reformation further than the Reformers, and said: Let us separate church and state, and have a free church made up of believers who are baptised into Christ Jesus by faith and in water. By God's grace, their principles came to this land of ours.

7

THE SEVENTEENTH CENTURY

One difference between 1600 and 1700 is of major importance for us: in 1600, 'nonconformist' Christians would not have been allowed to meet freely to worship as they chose, but in 1700 they could. We will see how that change occurred and how liberty of worship came to this land of ours so that for the last three hundred years or so we have been able to meet and worship as we felt we ought, with no one hindering us, no one dragging us off to prison, no one executing us because we did this. It is in this century that the battle was fought and finally won.

Now let me begin with the state of play at the beginning of the century. There were by this time three groups of professing Christians in England, three 'parties'. Officially there were no Roman Catholics. They had now been banned by law. If they were there, they were secret sympathisers.

There were two groups within the Church of England and one outside it. The two groups within the Church of England we call Anglicans and Puritans.

Anglicans accepted what Queen Elizabeth I virtually worked out as a kind of compromise, a mixture of things that used to be done by the Romans and things that the Reformers did, and the Anglican mixture was followed by many people in this country, particularly by those who regretted some of the Reformation.

But within the Church of England was another group of people, represented by Richard Baxter, who were called 'Puritans' because they desired to see a much purer Church of England. They wanted to abolish vestments, crucifixes and candles. They wanted worship to be plain, simple and pure. Above all, instead of worship being at the centre, they wanted the word of God to be at the centre. They were tremendous Bible readers. They did it in their own homes, as families. They did it, privately, as individuals. Above all, they wanted to see regular Bible study in the church.

Richard Baxter is a very good case in point. Not only did he provide two or three hours of Bible study on Sunday, but he had a rota and went from house to house giving twenty minutes to each family, just giving them Bible study. That was the secret of his effect on Kidderminster.

So here we have the Anglicans and the Puritans. The Anglicans still using quite a lot of the rites and ceremonies that had been used for centuries, and the Puritans, wanting to make it quite simple, as simple as it was in Geneva or Scotland, and to make the Church of England as simple as the Church of Scotland. Outside the Church of England was a third group who we call 'Independents' because they wanted to be independent of the church; they were called separatists because they separated from the church; they were called 'Brownists' because a man called Browne was a great leader among them, and, above all, they were called 'Congregationalists' because they believed that each congregation should order its own affairs under the Lord.

Here, then, is the 'state of play', at the beginning of the century. John Milton would be a fairly good case in point. The Congregationals or Independents rejected the idea of a national state church, and their slogan was 'Reformation, without tarrying for any'. In other words, we are not going to wait until they change the Parliament, or change the church. We are going to get right on ahead and live by the Bible in our local congregation. Of course, many of them paid for it with their lives, as did Greenwood and Barrowe. But that group grew.

We will look at the reign of each monarch in England over this century and ask what happened in England during this period. The funny thing is that a lot of it happened in Buckinghamshire – and a great deal happened in the Chilterns.

JAMES I

He had already been King of Scotland as James VI, but now he came south and became James I of England, and he had two ideas from the beginning which he had not spoken about publicly.

One was that he believed in the divine right of kings to rule religion. The second was that he believed in the divine right of bishops to rule the church. Now he kept very dark about this north of the border and the Scots were taken in. This rather shifty character, who could change overnight in his views apparently, deluded the Scots into thinking he would make a good king, and when he came south the English thought that he would follow the Puritan line, that he would purify the Church of England.

Very quickly they got a very big shock. He said, 'Presbyteries agree as well with monarchy as God and the devil' and his watchword for his reign in England was 'No bishop – no king'. There then began a most difficult period within the Church of England. James certainly took the side of the Anglicans very, very strongly and he wouldn't listen to government by representative bodies of believers. The king should rule the church and the bishop should rule the church, and he had a very good archbishop to help him in this.

Now to do this, in the year 1604 James called together a conference of leading Christians at Hampton Court (the palace where the maze is) where James ridiculed, insulted and laughed at the Puritans. He said, 'You are kill-joys. You don't like sports on Sundays. Right. I will make laws saying that it is perfectly alright to have sports and entertainment on Sundays.' He goaded them like this and what they went through in his ridicule was just nobody's business. We have an account of it.

But there was a Puritan present by the name of Reynolds, a famous professor from Oxford. He was a courteous, saintly gentleman, and all this ridicule and laughter did not disturb him one bit and he stood his ground. When James had run out of invective, Dr Reynolds said, 'Your majesty, I have a suggestion. It is about time we had a new English Bible.' This suggestion was taken up, almost to the surprise of King James, and from the Hampton Court conference, for seven years, people worked hard on this Bible. We have the King James Version, so-called not because he started the idea, or because he did it, but because he happened to be king at the time and it was presented to him on completion. We call it the 'Authorised Version' (also known, especially in the USA, as the King James Version). It came out in the year 1611. That year was momentous for England. The first Baptist church in England was founded in that same year.

Alas, following that Conference, King James issued a royal proclamation of conformity and said 'Every clergyman must accept the bishops. There must be complete conformity, complete uniformity right through the church.' Fifteen hundred clergy refused to sign it and three hundred of them were thrown into jail straight away. Others suffered. It was a major rift in the English church. At that time there came back into the Church of England vestments and rites and ceremonies which had not been seen since the beginning of the Reformation. They have remained ever since.

The result was that the Puritans made for Ireland. Some of them fled west and the Church of Ireland has always been nearer to the Reformation than the Church of England as a result. The Archbishop of Ireland at that time was Ussher, a great man for working out dates! If you have an Authorised Version that has at the head of Genesis 1 the year BC 4004 (which God never put in the Bible), you are looking at something that Ussher wrote. He it was who worked out that Adam appeared at about nine o'clock on October 21st in the year BC 4004. An English scholar said, rather dryly, 'Being a careful scholar he would not commit himself more fully than this!'

Archbishop Ussher was a grand archbishop and the Puritan clergymen tended to move west to Ireland, but the lay members of the church who were worried about James and who could not worship as they felt they should, fled east to the Netherlands. Many of the Independents, the Congregationals, fled to the Low Countries.

In the village of Scrooby in the northern part of Nottinghamshire, under a faithful pastor called John Robinson, a group of Independents met and formed their own congregation. Alas, the squire brought the magistrates and they were threatened with all sorts of things if they persisted in meeting. They finally decided that the only thing to do was to get a boat and go to Holland, where they could be free to worship. It is a most dramatic story of how they got the boats. They got a Dutch boat to come and meet from offshore, off Lincolnshire, near Boston. They set off from Boston Stump. They had two boats, one with the men in and one with the women and children in. They didn't come together so that the local magistrates wouldn't spot them. The two boats set off. The tragedy is that the boat with the women and children got stuck in the mud. The men reached the Dutch ship but then they saw on the shore British troops coming, who began to fire on the Dutch ship, and the ship had to pull off. The men saw their wives and children left on the mud and wondered what would happen. Fortunately, a year or two later, the wives and children were able to go out and meet them in Holland. There they met, free to worship God as they wished. In England under James you had to conform.

Something happened in Amsterdam. A group of Christians began to study the question of baptism. So far, as we have seen, all the main, or magisterial, Reformers practised infant baptism as it had been practised for centuries, but in Amsterdam a group under a man called Helwys began to look at this and they came to the far-reaching conclusion that baptism should be for believers only, and that that would say, more clearly than anything could say, that the church is made up of believers only.

Now, of course, they had no one to baptise them so two of them got together and one said, 'I will baptise you if you will baptise me.' This they did. Then, because they could not find work, they decided to risk coming back to London. In 1611 they came back, and in Spitalfields, London the first Baptist church in England was formed. Very soon they drew the attention of the authorities and they suffered for it.

A few years later a group of Independents, meeting in the Low Countries, who had stayed there, decided that it was just impracticable to stay in Europe. They were not understood. They couldn't get jobs. They were starving. They decided to do something tremendous. They decided to come back to England, to get hold of a ship, and go to the New World, and try to build in America a free world where people could worship without the state saying how they should. They came back to England and they persuaded the owner of the Mayflower to take them out.

THE PILGRIM FATHERS

In the village of Jordans, Buckinghamshire, in the Mayflower barn there are timbers which are claimed to be from the ship that took the Pilgrim Fathers, in 1620, from Plymouth away out to New England, to the New World. What a hard experience awaited them there. In the first winter half of them died. There was coldness, and lack of food and medical help. But they stayed, and even though they had battles with established Anglican areas, the Pilgrim Fathers began something which means that today America is entirely free of any state/church relationship, and where anybody may worship as they feel they ought. That is one of the reasons why most of the unusual sects seem to start in America. They were free to do so. That was the risk they ran, but they would rather run the risk of that and have religious liberty than try and stamp out by force of law what didn't fit in with their ideas of religion.

CHARLES I

Charles I, alas, was one worse than his predecessor James I, and I am afraid, believing this divine right of kings and bishops, he went much further. Find a Puritan, into prison with him! Fine him heavily, put him in the pillory, cut his ears off, slit his nose – all this was going on in the reign of Charles I.

Archbishop Laud of Canterbury, at this time, helped Charles I to turn the clock back. The communion table in the parish church was now called again the altar, and now people were told to bow to it. Parliament objected, so Charles I did without a Parliament for eleven years! Can you imagine a king or queen today doing that? Fifteen thousand Londoners marched on the Palace and presented to King Charles I the 'Root and Branch

Petition'. If you have ever heard of the phrase 'root and branch', this is where it comes from. They wanted all Romish superstition rooted out, root and branch. Charles I refused to listen, and within a very short time England was at civil war.

The war broke out in 1642. Parliament was fighting the king, and it was a religious issue. By and large, the Anglicans fought with the king and the Puritans fought with Parliament. By and large, the north and the west was in the king's hands and the south and the east was in the Parliament's hands. That is why, if you study the distribution of Free churches today, you will find that it follows that pattern.

The border came between Aylesbury and Oxford. One of the greatest fighters for the Parliament was John Hampden, and not far from a church of which I was pastor is Hampden Road, and one of my children was in the Hampden house in the local school. If you go to Aylesbury there, standing in the square is a statue of Hampden, whose home was near Stoke Mandeville. Alas, that leader was killed very early in the war, and Parliament began to lose the battle.

They were waiting for a leader. Oliver Cromwell blended them in to a 'New Model Army'. Under the famous catchphrase 'Trust in God and keep your powder dry', he put new morale into the troops fighting for religious liberty. There met in Westminster at this time, during the civil war, a group of clergymen and scholars from Oxford and Cambridge, to try and work out some kind of a pattern of church life that would be acceptable to all. It was called The Westminster Assembly of Divines, and there were a few Scots invited who seemed to influence them terribly heavily, as Scots often do. They produced a creed of their beliefs called the Westminster Confession of Faith, and to this very day, this is the confession of faith not only for the Scottish, but for most Presbyterians in the world. I am sure you could quote one thing from the Catechism based on it: 'What is the chief end of man? The chief end of man is to glorify God and enjoy Him forever.' The Scots accepted it but the English never did.

Charles I was still around but was finally brought to London to be beheaded. He was kept for a short time in the Manor House at Stoke Poges. There, above the fireplace, painted on the plaster wall, is the royal coat of arms of Charles. To while away the hours and keep his mind off his execution he painted his royal coat of arms on the plaster.

Among the soldiers who fought with Oliver Cromwell, was a hard drinking, hard fighting, hard swearing young man, who had been born at a little village called Elstow, near Bedford. His name was John Bunyan.

After the Civil War, the Presbyterians gained control of the Church of England and tried to make everybody a Presbyterian. Isn't it funny? When the Anglicans are in control everybody must be Anglican. When the Presbyterians get it, everybody must be Presbyterian – which caused someone to say that new Presbyter was but old priest writ large. In other words, we have just changed one tyranny for another.

CHARLES II

One could hardly say things bad enough about this unprincipled profligate who was accepted by the Scots first – and they crowned him at Scone, on the Stone of Scone, thinking that he would fight with the Scots and the Parliament of England for Presbyterianism, for a purer Puritan church. Alas, the Scots regretted their folly very quickly. I cannot go into the story of the Covenanters; suffice to say, that 17,000 Scottish Covenanters, meeting in secret in the Highlands to worship God as they felt they ought, suffered under Charles II.

Back in England, Charles II was a secret sympathiser with the Roman Catholic church. His ambition was, by intrigue, to bring them back. He made a secret treaty with Louis XIV of France, to turn the clock back two hundred years to the Pre-Reformation days. How did he do it? 1661 began a series of Acts of Parliament to turn the clock back. 1662 was the worst. It was called the Act of Uniformity. It was not Roman, yet, but it was Anglican and Charles II was saying, and Parliament was saying 'Everybody must be this'. It was in that year, 1662, that nearly two thousand clergymen left their livings and went out into the unknown without home, job or anything else because they refused to conform to the Act of Uniformity, and into the English language came the new word 'nonconformist'. That word was a criminal word at the beginning. A nonconformist ran tremendous risks and one of those turned out at that time was Richard Baxter. In 1665 another law was enacted by Parliament called the Five Mile Act, because expelled clergy were creeping back secretly, to hold meetings with their own people. No clergyman was to be allowed within five miles of his former church.

Interestingly, if you go to Wendover, you will see the Baptist church on the right hand side of the road. It is a good five minutes' walk from the village. You might wonder: why build a church outside a village? The answer is very simple. In 1662, the vicar of Aylesbury was turned out because he refused to conform. He kept creeping back into Aylesbury, holding meetings in kitchens and gardens and anywhere he could, but then the Five Mile Act was passed. Do you know what he did? He stood in the middle of Aylesbury and he started walking out five miles. He paced it out and five miles brought him to a field and he started meetings in the field and people walked five miles from Aylesbury. They erected a place of worship which is now the Baptist church of Wendover. It is exactly five miles away!

In 1673 came the notorious Test Act. The result was that Parliament was saying there must be neither Roman Catholic nor nonconformist in

England. Everybody must worship one way. That caused a great deal of suffering.

John Bunyan was converted through listening to the gossip of some housewives in a backyard. If you gossip in a backyard, just bear in mind you might reach a John Bunyan if you are gossiping about the right things – because this hard drinking, swearing, fighting young man, overheard some women talking about Jesus. He had never heard anything so sweet, and it convicted him of his sin. He was converted and became a preacher in Bedford. He was baptised as a believer and he preached the gospel wherever he could.

Bunyan was thrown into prison in the reign of Charles II. Twelve years he was in prison, with only one break. He was separated from his blind wife and his children and suffering privation, but one day in the jail he had a dream. He dreamt he saw a man with a burden on his back and a man who wanted to get rid of his burden. He began to write down the dream – and that dream is *The Pilgrim's Progress*. I hope you have read that book right through in the adult version and not in the children's version. The adult version gives you not just what happened to Pilgrim but what he thought and what he said. I hope that some day you will also read another important book by John Bunyan, *Grace Abounding to the Chief of Sinners*. It describes his conversion and how he became the preacher that he was. I suppose Bunyan's *Pilgrim's Progress* is the best known Christian book, next to the Bible.

He never mentioned the church in it. He never mentioned the sacraments in it and therefore it was accepted by Christians of all churchmanship, and to this very day it has had one of the widest appeals in the Christian world of any book ever written. He died in 1688. 'Bishop Bunyan' they called him by the end of his life, but the one thing he didn't want to be was a bishop. As he travelled around and as people came to him for help they said, 'You've got as much right to be called a bishop as they have, so we are going to call you that.' So 'Bishop Bunyan' he was.

Another man who suffered during this time was George Fox, who had a very deep, religious experience in the year 1646. Now there was something very good about that experience and something not so good. George Fox discovered, or rather rediscovered, the power of the Holy Spirit to 'guide into all truth'. He called this experience 'the inner Light'. He said, 'It is no use just having the holy scripture outside you or even in your head. You need the Holy Spirit inside you as well.' Now that was something that needed to be rediscovered and needed to be said. You can have the holy scripture off pat, but without the Holy Spirit it is dead. It is not alive. George Fox rediscovered the Holy Spirit.

Alas, having rediscovered something good, he then went and said something not so good. He went one step further and said that the 'sure word of prophecy which we need today is not the scriptures but the Holy Spirit alone'. Alas, from that statement has come the greatest weakness of the movement that followed this man. For this man gathered around him a group of people of similar outlook whom they called 'The Society of Friends'. Other people nicknamed them 'Quakers' because they quaked and trembled before God in their meetings. Their strength is that they believed that God can speak inwardly through the Holy Spirit, their weaknesses that they rejected the sacraments which the Lord Jesus meant them to have, because they are 'outward', and a tendency to disregard the scripture and rely entirely on inner thoughts.

Fox, imprisoned for saying that, because of its unorthodoxy, incidentally, suffered greatly. At one time during the reign of Charles II there were 4000 Quakers in prison. If you can imagine what proportion that was, you can understand their sufferings, especially when you consider that in prison you got no food unless friends brought it to you, and if you put all the Quakers in prison there would be nobody to bring them food.

A young aristocrat said, 'We will never get freedom in England to worship as we ought. We must go to the New World.' William Penn lies buried, with his family, in the quiet little burial ground of Jordans Meeting House. But William Penn went to the New World and pressed beyond the frontiers of the colonies of the eastern seaboard, and he said, 'We will have a state of religious liberty'. It became known as Pennsylvania – the colony of William Penn, where they might be free to worship and follow the inner light of the Holy Spirit. He crossed the Atlantic three or four times but finally died in England.

JAMES II

James II was an avowed Roman Catholic who, not in any subtle way like Charles II but in a completely open way, said, 'I will get you back to Rome if it kills me.' To do this, he used the notoriously brutal Judge Jeffreys of Bulstrode Park, Gerrards Cross, with his infamous acts. It was too much for England and as a result of a popular rising against the king, James II had to flee.

WILLIAM AND MARY

William and Mary came to the throne of England and a new era of stability and tolerance began, an era that set the pattern for the rest of English history, as far as church life goes, with one exception.

The Roman Catholics were not allowed back in this reign and they weren't allowed back for another hundred years, but tolerance was extended to others. In 1689, nonconformists were at least partially recognised and the persecutions began to cease. I have a book written by Foxe called *Foxe's Book of Martyrs*. It was required reading for children on Sunday in the time of my great grandfather. I don't know that I would dare to give it to my children now or I would have my children's teacher after me for filling their minds with such things. It is the most horrible account of Christian martyrs, from the time of the New Testament through to 1682. I fear that the author hoped that no more stories of martyrdom would need to be written, after *Foxe's Book of Martyrs*, and that the tolerance gained towards the end of that century, would be lasting and that there would be no more.

In a sense there haven't been any more martyrs in England, but over the world there has not been a period of ten years since Jesus died on the cross when Christians have not died for the faith – and still it goes on, somewhere in the world. However, in England, toleration came, and for the first time nonconformists could put up buildings of worship, after the passage of William and Mary's Toleration Act of 1689. By the end of the century nonconformists had 1000 places of worship.

So now this was the position: Anglicanism is still the Established Religion. The Puritans have largely left the Anglican church, having either gone to Ireland or to America, or they have gone into the Independents or the Baptists and become nonconformists. In 1662, two thousand more Anglicans came out and joined the nonconformists. By the end of the century, nonconformist chapels and meeting houses were everywhere in the south-east of England and spreading into the north and west.

That was the overall position, but within the Anglican church there were three parties. So as I gave you the 'state of play' at 1600, let me give you the 'state of parties' at 1700. The parties in the Church of England remain to this day: high, broad and low. They are right there at the end of the seventeenth century.

The high party still hanker after the Romish practices in worship. The low party belongs really to the few Puritans who managed to stay in somehow and who had very simple, unadorned worship without the vestments, without the altar, with just a table, and who worshipped very much like the Church of Scotland and were very doubtful about having bishops. The broad party is the one that I want to leave you thinking about because it is the beginning of the eighteenth century story.

Can I ask this question: what did God think about all this? And what did the devil think about all this? I have the feeling that the devil was laughing up his sleeve at Christians killing each other. I have the feeling he was thrilled that, physically, they were destroying each other. But when the Toleration Act came and people allowed each other to worship freely, the devil had to think up a new tactic and he thought up a most devilish one: instead of destroying Christians physically, he would think up something that would destroy them mentally.

During the seventeenth century some very odd ideas had been produced on the continent in the name of Christianity. In Sweden, a scientist called Swedenborg was producing some incredible ideas and calling them Christianity, founding the 'New

Jerusalem Church'. You may not have come across those. I found more of them in Lancashire.

On the continent, Socinus, in Italy, was saying this kind of thing:'The Bible is not the word of God. It is helpful but it's not just the word of God like that; Jesus was not the Son of God; he was simply a great man of God; we must imitate his example. Jesus didn't die for our sins, he died to give us an example of love.' This was being said, and these ideas were coming across the English Channel.

There were other ideas from Arminius of Holland, who opposed the teaching of Calvin. Ever since we have had Calvinism and Arminianism. Calvinism emphasised the sovereignty and the will of God. Arminianism emphasised the free will of man. They came almost to mental blows over this difference.

Into the Church of England, from the continent, was coming a party of people who really felt that, as long as you went to church and worshipped, it didn't really matter whether you held the old beliefs. Until the end of the seventeenth century, the people who disagreed about church order, about bishops, about baptism were all agreed about Christian beliefs and what the gospel was, but now there came into the Church of England from the continent a party that believed you could be much more latitudinarian in your doctrine. In other words, you could be wider, broader in your thinking than the old-fashioned gospel. This was to almost kill the Church of England by the 1730s. Spiritually, it was to rob that church of its power and heritage.

I have told you all this, not because I want to give you a history lesson but because I want you to realise that if we were living in the 1700s, you and I would not have been free to worship as we chose. We would have had to 'conform'. You would have to conform to a set order of service settled by Act of Parliament. You would have had to conform to a rigid church government settled by Act of Parliament and there would be no freedom for you to meet to decide what the Lord would have us do. This liberty is now ours. Thank the Lord that there were those who saw that the New Testament demanded a free church in a free state, and that religion was a matter of conscience – those who carried this to the New World, those who went to the continent with this idea, but above all, those who stayed in England and went to prison and fought it out. This means that you and I might worship God as we feel our conscience dictates.

The price of liberty is eternal vigilance. We could lose that liberty again, very easily. Others lost it. We have not only to look back into the past, but to praise God that in the future he can keep us where we ought to be.

I have also told you this story to tell you this: that in spite of all these battles, and in spite of these difficulties, the church of God goes on, and in every generation the Holy Spirit converts men and women and makes them blazing preachers of the gospel and sends them out, and even in spite of all that happened the church was still there,

Christians were still there, the gospel was still there, the Bible was still there – for Jesus said, 'I will build *my* church and the gates of hell shall not prevail against it.'

8

THE EIGHTEENTH CENTURY

In November 1699, just a few weeks before the eighteenth century opened, *Gulliver's Travels* was published. It was written by Jonathan Swift, an Irishman who tried to settle many times in England but failed to do so, and finally died insane in Dublin. His book was a savage attack on English society at the beginning of the eighteenth century and it is not a children's book. If you want to know what England was like at the beginning of this period, read that book. A few years later, Robinson Crusoe found his island. It seems there was a craze at that time to get out of England, away from English society, and Robinson Crusoe seems much happier on his desert island than when he comes back to England in the year 1715.

These two books introduce a fact we must mention before we look at the church, and that is that England was going to pieces. Socially, England was in a bad way and we must ask why – what caused this? Can I sum up what I want to say in a rather simple and maybe crude way, by saying that man was turning on the cold tap and God was turning on the hot tap, through the eighteenth century.

Man was turning on the cold tap of what we call rationalism, the intellect by itself, reason. And God was turning on the hot tap of what we call revivalism. He was calling some great men to preach the gospel and to lift the temperature of English society.

First, the cold tap, and if you get this kind of 'deadness' creeping over you, that is precisely what was creeping over English society. People were going spiritually dead and the reason was that their beliefs were going in the wrong direction and therefore their behaviour went in the wrong direction.

One of the lessons we learn from the eighteenth century is that a man's beliefs affect his behaviour. What a man thinks in his heart, so he will be in his outward life. So what kind of beliefs were 'cooling' religion? What kind of beliefs were killing English society at the beginning of the eighteenth century? It was partly the influence of science. There had been many wonderful discoveries. Copernicus had discovered (or at least had said that) the planets revolved around the sun and not the earth, and Galileo, with his telescope, had discovered that this was in fact so. Isaac Newton was still discovering things about apples and greater laws illustrated thereby and was propounding the law of gravity. Above all, Francis Bacon and Descartes were saying that the universe in which we live is governed by laws which cannot be broken. In other words, if an apple comes off your apple tree, it must come down. That is a law of gravity. It could never be broken. They were saying that these laws are absolutely fixed. Now that, of course, with one blow, sweeps out miracle and it sweeps out a great deal of the things that happened in the Bible, for some of the things that happened in the Bible seem to go right against such natural laws.

Furthermore, Francis Bacon said this (and you would be amazed when I say this, to realise how modern he was and how much we are indebted or influenced by him) – the only things that you can say are true are the things that you can prove by observation and if you can't prove a thing scientifically, by observation, you must not believe it. You must not accept anything on authority. You must always test it and if you can't prove it scientifically, by observation, you need not believe it. That was a tremendous step forward or backward, depending on which way you look at it. But it is astonishing how school pupils today may say, 'I can't believe it unless you can prove it. I can't believe in God unless you can demonstrate him, unless I can observe him. I can't believe in heaven, or in the devil. You can't prove these things scientifically.' Now they are just echoing what Francis Bacon was saying and, frankly, that idea kills religion dead. It is bound to, because you cannot prove the eternal realm by observation.

So then, where does God fit in? Did this mean that they ceased to believe in God in the eighteenth century? No! But many switched from a belief that we call theism to a belief we call deism, which is one step on the way to atheism.

Quite simply, theism is the belief that God created the world and controls it. Deism is the belief that God created the world but can't control it. Atheism is the belief that he didn't create it either because there isn't a God to create!

Now I could find out whether you were a deist or not by asking you whether you would ever pray about the weather. That would tell me straight away whether you believe that God controls the world he has made. If you believe that God created and controls the world he has made, then you are a theist. I am a theist and the Bible is a theistic book.

But in the eighteenth century, it began to be said: 'If the universe is governed by these hard laws and you can't break them, then God may have made them but there is nothing that can be done about it now, so there is no point in asking him to change anything and to step in and do something. You can still believe in God but he is a God who made it long ago and then just left it running.'

One of the most popular ideas, propounded by a bishop, was that the world is like a gigantic clock. Once you have made it there is nothing you can do about it. Once you have wound it up, it will just go on according to its own laws. I can't say to a clock 'Here, just a minute. Go backwards or stop!'

It is a mechanism governed by its laws. The deists believed that God made the world and wound it up, and then he has just got to sit back. There is nothing more he can do about it. There is a God but he can't do anything.

That is really a dead sort of God and you wouldn't pray much to a God who couldn't do anything, would you? This was killing prayer and it was killing belief in a living God who was still in control of everything. Now this sort of thinking – that God was a long way off and couldn't do much – crept right in to the churches. It was called by different names in different churches. In the Church of England they called it latitudinarianism. In the Church of Scotland they called it moderatism. In the Baptists, they called it unitarianism because one of the beliefs was that God could not possibly have come down to earth, and Jesus must therefore just have been a great man.

So the faith, watered down, began to disappear, and all denominations suffered from this. Some Baptist churches closed down because of this kind of thinking. Worship became very formal and very dead. You just came to pay respects to the deity who made it all but you must never expect him to do anything! God couldn't, they thought, he is outside what he has made.

Not only did they discover, as they thought, laws of nature, there were other writers who discovered, as they thought, laws of society. John Locke was writing about laws governing society, as was

Voltaire in the age of Louis XIV. Another was the Frenchman Rousseau, and his saying 'Man is born free and everywhere he is in chains' is a typical Rousseau saying. Then there was the Scotsman Adam Smith, who wrote a very big tome on how to 'balance your imports and your exports' and 'division of labour'. That is strangely 'modern' too. There was Mary Wollstonecraft and she was fighting for the 'divine rights' (you might almost call it!) of women. She wrote a long book in which she advocated women voting and in which she advocated playing grounds at schools, co-education which was revolutionary in those days, and division into secondary modern and grammar. She was quite a fighter, and many of the ideas in her book have come about.

These were all trying to discover 'laws of society', and trying to discover how society 'ticks'. But they were all saying much the same thing: that the laws of society don't need God any more than the laws of nature. The world of nature runs without God and the world of society, and of human nature, runs without God as well – and it was from such ideas the French Revolution came. Rousseau has been called 'the father of the French Revolution'.

Now the church tried to fight back using the weapons of the intellect. Bishop Butler and Bishop Berkeley really tried to preach intellectually. They really tried to match the evidence against God with evidence for God, and they made the whole thing a bit of an intellectual argument. Quite frankly, that never did much good. You can never argue a person into spiritual life. You might remove some of their questions and the barriers but you will never build a church on intellectual argument alone.

That the beliefs of the eighteenth century were somewhat cold and intellectual was bound to have a tremendous effect on behaviour. The century was a time of turmoil; there was a wind of change when societies were turning upside down.

In America it was the age of the revolt of the American colonies and the founding of the United States and Jefferson wrote Locke's 'Philosophy', his laws of society, into the Declaration of Independence. If you read Locke's book first and then the Declaration of Independence, you will find where the United States got their Declaration from.

In France in July 1789, all these ideas burst up into the French Revolution. Now 'reason' was going to be the goddess, and on the very altar of the Cathedral of Notre Dame in Paris they enthroned the goddess of reason, and said, 'No more God', and the reign of terror began. Later, Napoleon was to enter Rome, confiscate the papal territories and bring the Pope as a prisoner to France – this was the kind of turmoil.

What happened in England with all this turmoil of ideas? The answer is: precious little. England just drifted down while everybody else had a revolution. Again, quite typically English perhaps. We just let things slide while other countries are being turned upside down. But slide they did! In religion there was a hearty dislike of what was called 'enthusiasm'. Nowadays we would say 'emotionalism' – it is the same word. People went to church and said, 'No emotionalism in church, no enthusiasms, no fanaticism, just a nice intellectual talk from the vicar, but no getting excited, no getting worked up, no showing any feelings.' Now of course that is not a balanced religion, and lethargy and apathy crept into the congregations. A century ago they went to fight for religion. Now they just sat in the pew and yawned! Religion, I am afraid, became very much the religion of the upper class. The working man was poor, ignorant and just not welcome.

When offered the position of Archbishop of Canterbury, Butler said, 'It is too late for me to save a dying church. It will have disappeared in my lifetime.' That was the state of the church, and where the spiritual state is like that, the moral state will be worse.

If you wanted to spend an afternoon out in the eighteenth century you got your family together and you went up to Tyburn – now known as Hyde Park Corner, near Marble Arch. There, if you look around Marble Arch today, you will see a triangle of stones embedded in the road, and there on that triangle there was a gallows. You went there, and took a picnic and you watched people being hanged. It was great fun. Children, women, men – you could be hanged for stealing five shillings' worth of goods or a shilling in money, and if you wanted amusement you went to Hyde Park Corner not to hear the speakers, but to watch the hangings. If you wanted another amusement, you went to a cockpit and you saw the cockfighting, and of course, the quickest way out of London and the other industrial areas, was the public house and drink was cheap. The advertisements hanging in the lanes of London just simply read, 'Drunk for a penny, dead drunk for twopence. Free straw to lie on.' Now I know that a penny was a penny in those days and two pence was two pence, but this, of course, led to the most appalling abuses.

Not only was there heavy drinking and heavy gambling, there was heavy fighting, and if you want to study the social life of England as it became during this dead, cold, intellectual period, then read a book like Fielding's *Tom Jones*. Isn't it interesting that this has been made into a film? The whole story is coming up again and the wheels are turning. But 'Tom Jones' is a typical book of the immorality of those days. Or study Hogarth's paintings, the cartoons of *A Rake's Progress*. You will see it there. Or read Boswell's *Life of Samuel Johnson* if you want to see a taste of higher society, but this is the eighteenth century.

One man writing at the time summed it all up by saying this: 'Decay in religion, licentiousness in morals, public corruption and profaneness of language.' That was England in the first thirty or forty years of that century. It is no wonder that Edward Gibbon was busy writing *The Decline and*

Fall of the Roman Empire. It is surprising he didn't go on to write of the decline and fall of English society. He could easily have done so.

What stopped England from having a revolution? Why did the poor not rise? Why wasn't there a complete turning upside down of society? What stopped England going through the turmoil that America went through, that France went through? What was the factor here that altered the course of our history? The fact is that during this century God 'turned on the hot tap'. I am finished with all the cold stuff and the intellectual stuff now. God turned on the breath of revival. The Holy Spirit did the most amazing things in this land of ours, from which we are still benefiting.

God's method is always to choose a person and to fill that person with his Holy Spirit and to enable them to do it. It is very rarely that God has worked through committees, or larger groups of people. His method is always to raise up people to do the job. It always will be so, and those called need to remain in a right relationship to Christ.

From Wales, he raised up Howell Harris, Griffith Jones and Daniel Rowlan during this century and they changed the course of Welsh history.

From America, it was in this century that he raised up Theodore Frelinghuysen. He in turn influenced the great preacher Jonathan Edwards and David Brainerd, a great man of prayer who went as a missionary to the Indians and died after only three years but changed American history.

These men were raised up and it is estimated that in the eighteenth century, in America alone, 300,000 people were led to the Lord, and considering the population then, that is quite a revival, with the camp meetings flourishing at the end of the century.

But the two countries we need to mention now are, first of all, Germany and then England, because they are closely related. God raised up in Germany Count von Zinzendorf, who had a huge estate in Saxony called Herrnhut, and to that estate there came one day some beggars. They were worshippers of the Lord Jesus Christ. They were the remains of the church of Jan Hus in Bohemia, and still, centuries after Jan Hus, they met simply around the Lord Jesus Christ. They had been turned out of their country and they came to Count von Zinzendorf (and he had been converted a short time before), and he said, 'Come on in. You can have my estate. You can build houses here. I will protect you and together we will build up a Christian community' – and they did. They called it the Moravian community. They were the first real missionary society in Europe. There had been other attempts at missionary work, but that little group of Moravians sent out no fewer than 25 missionaries in the first few years of their life, to take the gospel of Christ to the uttermost parts of the earth. They went to America, they came to England. There is a Moravian church just below the Alexandra Palace in North London. You will find Moravians here and there in this country and in America and throughout the world. Count Zinzendorf, who started that, was to have a profound influence on England through a friend of his.

By the way, if you want to know the hymns of Count von Zinzendorf, here are two: *Jesus still lead on till our rest be won*; *Jesus, Thy blood and righteousness*. Count von Zinzendorf once said this: 'I have only one passion. It is Jesus'. That sums up his life. No wonder he was the great man he was.

How did God turn the hot tap on in England? How did he raise the spiritual temperature? The answer again is that he did it through individuals. He laid his hand on George Whitefield, a young man working his way through Oxford by cleaning the shoes of the students. He was a young man who was going places, a young man who was a hard worker. He was a disciplined young man, but God said, 'You are a sinner and you need salvation', and, through a great spiritual struggle, George Whitefield came to know the Lord Jesus Christ and he began to preach. A year after his conversion he was preaching in Gloucester and his text was 2 Corinthians 5:17 – *If any man be in Christ he is a new creature*. When he preached that sermon he said this, which mortally offended most of his hearers: 'I do not care if you have been baptised. I do not care if you have had water on your forehead in the name of the Trinity. You must be born again!' He said, 'I've got the new birth and I want you to have it.' When he finished preaching seventeen people were born again. That was the beginning. He was soon preaching to thirty and forty thousand people at once. He not only travelled England. He went to Scotland and preached to forty thousand in Edinburgh, and then he crossed the Atlantic thirteen times, and died in America at the end, but he was preaching everywhere he could go. George Whitefield was one of the greatest servants of God England has seen.

The tragedy is that most of his work disappeared after his death because he never organised follow-up for his converts. The only person who really urged him to start churches in a sense was the Countess of Huntingdon. If ever you have seen a church with the words displayed 'Countess of Huntingdon's Connexion' you are going back to the days of that lady who supported George Whitefield. But when he died he said, 'I feel my work has been a rope of sand and will disappear very quickly.' In fact it has done and you don't hear of any Whitefieldites. You don't hear of any groups today except the Countess of Huntingdon's Connexion church and one or two other small groups. Nevertheless, he led thousands to the Lord. I don't mean that they fell away. I mean that they found their way into other churches.

John Wesley's story begins in the little village of Epworth, Lincolnshire, where, as it happens, I was married in the Wesley Memorial church. The minister who conducted our wedding was the warden of the Old Rectory which was the home of the Wesley family. There in that Rectory something happened and something new was born, away up in the flat country of Lincolnshire on that little island that just rises up to Epworth.

Now John Wesley's grandparents had been Independents, which explains a great deal, but his parents were both Anglican by conviction and they were there as the Vicar and his wife of that little town of Epworth. We need to consider the parents.

Samuel Wesley was quite an amazing man, a bit of a poet. He spent most of his years writing a poem on Job which was never really popular, but he passed on to his sons a poetic gift. But the mother, Susannah Wesley, was amazing. She had nineteen children, twelve of whom she reared! She trained them not to cry after they were one year old. When they were five she taught them to read until by the end of their first week they could read Genesis 1. How much they understood I don't know and how she did it I don't know. None of your modern toys and other things to help them. She gave one hour a week to each child to help them grow spiritually, and when you study the life of Susannah Wesley, you have studied the beginning of Methodism, for that is what was to come.

When John (or Jackie, as she called him) was seven years old, the Rectory caught fire and they got all the children out bar one – Jackie, little John. There was a dramatic moment when they saw him at the upstairs window. The villagers climbed on each other's backs to rescue him, and she clutched him to her bosom and said, 'You are a brand plucked from the burning,' and she believed from then on that John would be her greatest son, and so he was.

John went to Charterhouse school and then to Oxford to join his brother Charles. There they formed what they called the 'Holy Club' and my, it was, and it was offensive too, to everybody else, as such a name might indicate. They got up at four in the morning to pray. They did their studies as students during the day and then they visited the jail. They had a Dispensary to give medicines to sick people, and they were trying desperately to save themselves by being good.

One member of the Holy Club was George Whitefield, and that is where their paths crossed. This little group of students were desperately trying to get to heaven by being good. They still hadn't learned how you become a Christian. They were so methodical in the way they got up and went to the jail and did this, that and the other and kept accounts of all that they did, that the students didn't call them the Holy Club but gave them a nickname: 'Methodists!,' they said. It was a term of abuse but the nickname stuck and has stuck to this very day.

The time came when John realised that he still felt he wasn't doing enough for God, so he offered for the ministry as his father had before him and as his brother had before him. John and Charles were ordained by the Archbishop of Canterbury and they were now priests of the Church of England and were still not Christians, and because they knew this in their heart, they felt they weren't doing enough for God so they volunteered to go out as missionaries to Georgia, to the Red Indians. They thought: 'Surely if you go as a missionary you get saved?' and they went out to save their own souls. Now could you get as far as that without being a Christian? Of course you can, and they did, and they were not only priests, they were missionaries and they hadn't saved their own souls and they were desperately trying to.

On the way out, in the middle of the Atlantic, they struck a storm and were all frightened. They panicked and they thought the end had come. They threw things overboard to lighten the ship but it looked as if all was lost. But there in the middle of the ship was a group of people, quiet, calm, praying, Moravian refugees from Herrnhut who knew Count von Zinzendorf. John Wesley went up to them afterwards, in his clergyman's garb and said, 'Why weren't you afraid?' and they said, 'Why should we be?' One of them began to ask him about his soul and said, 'Do you know that Jesus is your Saviour?' This clergyman, John Wesley replied, 'I know he is the Saviour of the world'. 'But do you know that he is your Saviour?' And John Wesley said 'Yes' but in his diary that night he admitted it was a lie and said, 'I go to Georgia to save my own soul. How can I save the souls of the Indians?'

He came back to London after three miserable years of failure and wondered what he should do. His brother came back too, an equal failure, but praise God, God had someone waiting in London for him, a man called Peter Bohler. He was another Moravian from Count von Zinzendorf. Peter Bohler got hold of them and he talked to them. Then, one never-to-be-forgotten Sunday, John Wesley went to St Paul's Cathedral to worship, and as he read his Bible that morning, he read these words: 'Thou art not far from the kingdom of God.'

That night he went to a little meeting of the Moravian Germans in Aldersgate Street. There is a bank there now but they have put a plate to show where it took place and in Aldersgate Street on May 24th 1738 he went to the meeting and they read aloud Luther's commentary on Romans. I wonder how many people would stand much of that in church today – reading a commentary on Romans, aloud, for some hours. But when the clock said 'a quarter to nine' at night, John Wesley said, 'I felt my heart strangely warmed. I felt I did trust in Christ, Christ alone, for salvation; and an assurance was given me, that he had taken away my sins, even mine, and saved me from the law of sin and death.' An assurance was given him at that moment that he really was a forgiven sinner. Now here he was, a failed missionary, an ordained priest in the Church of England. He had done all those good things for other people and yet he didn't know his sins were forgiven. That is what happens when you try to save yourself, because you are putting your trust in what you do instead of what Christ does, and this was the one thing he couldn't learn.

By the way, my son is named Richard Wesley because he was born at a quarter to nine on a Sunday evening, as well as the fact that he was born in Lincolnshire, not far from Epworth and that his old dad thought a lot of John Wesley.

Now John went almost straight away out to Germany to visit von Zinzendorf and he came back with many of their hymns and translated them into English. He came back wanting to preach the gospel, and preach it, he did, but pulpits closed to him. Every time he preached in the Church of England, they told him after the service 'That is your first and last visit here' and so he finally was in a position where he couldn't preach!

Then George Whitefield said to him, 'John, will you come and preach in the open air?' and John Wesley thought it was the most dreadful thing in the world, for an ordained clergyman not to preach from a pulpit! But then he remembered that Christ preached his Sermon on the Mount and he said, 'Well, if Christ could preach on a mountain, so can I' and he went down to Kingswood, outside Bristol, to the miners. He preached, and as he preached, he described in his Journal how the tears made little white rivers down their black cheeks!

John Wesley realised that God was calling him to the same ministry as George Whitefield, who was now leaving for America and he took up the threads of George Whitefield's preaching. It was in April 1739 that he began open air preaching. Mind you, he had opposition. There were times when he was dragged by the hair through the streets, as in the Wednesbury riots, but in fifty years he travelled a quarter of a million miles on horseback with a Bible in his hand and a horse between his knees. He would ride into a village and preach, and this is how he preached. He would begin by preaching the Ten Commandments and he would preach the law by which every man and woman will be judged, and he would go on preaching the law for days until people began to look unhappy and until they began to look troubled. Then, when he realised they were beginning to realise they were sinners, he says in his diary 'I began to mix a bit of the love of God with the law of God and a bit more and a bit more until finally I was preaching the gospel of the love of God.'

Now Wesley discovered that you cannot preach the love of God until you have preached the law; that there is no point in preaching the Saviour until you have preached sin. What comfort can a Saviour bring to those who never felt their woe? That was written all over his ministry.

Mind you, it was an unusual and curious sight to see a Church of England clergyman, still with all his vestments, standing in the middle of a village green, preaching like that. They had never seen anything like it, but he went to the working man.

His three centres were London, Bristol and Newcastle, and all over that 'triangle' you will find places where Wesley preached. His last sermon was preached at Leatherhead in Surrey and there is a tablet on the Town Hall now.

He preached everywhere on the principle, as he said, 'The world is my parish.' There may be a little element of truth in the suggestion that he was helped in his travels by an unhappy marriage, and kept on the move. That was the only real shadow over his life but there are many who felt grateful for it, that he was travelling. He travelled and travelled and he preached and he preached. Seven times a day was normal.

Not only did he preach but he wrote, and published books and pamphlets. He started schools and orphanages. He opened dispensaries. He was the first to use electric treatment for rheumatism with a machine which you can see in City Road today, in his house, and they discovered it produces enough electricity to kill a man, but he used it for rheumatism!

He was a most varied man but quite obviously it soon became apparent that he couldn't do all this himself and the trouble was that he had few clergymen to do it with him, so his mother came up with the idea. She said, 'What about unordained preachers, lay preachers, local preachers who would not go around as you do, but preach locally?'

One of the very first team of six was John Pawson, and his wife Frances was one of the leading Methodist women of that day, so I suppose our tribal association goes way back to the beginning! So with a team, John Wesley's reply to his mother was 'Give me a hundred of such men. We'll set

England on fire!' and they did, and when he died there were 80,000 people meeting in fellowship as a result of his travels.

Now he did not do what George Whitefield did, or at least he did do what George Whitefield didn't. When they were converted he built them up into fellowships, largely because the local churches wouldn't have them. So he would build them into, not churches, but he called them societies – Methodist Societies. He gave them class leaders whose job it was to lead them spiritually. Then he had so many societies in a district, and he called that district a circuit, because a local preacher could go round a circuit on horseback once a month and preach in every place.

This kind of set up is still used today though I think it is very ill adapted to modern times. For horseback it is a very good idea and for the kind of setting in which he was, it was an ideal piece of organisation. So he built them into an organisation.

Bear in mind that all this time John Wesley was a Church of England clergyman. What did they think about him? Well, I am afraid they thought very badly about him, especially when he ordained ministers for America! Though he never left the Church of England it was quite obvious that as soon as he died the Methodist societies would become Methodist churches and this they did, and the split came as soon as he died. But I think John Wesley was to blame, or at least was the man who did all that needed to be done to separate, and I like the remark of someone who said, 'John Wesley was like a man rowing a boat. He kept his face towards the Church of England but every pull of his oars took him further from it.'

So we are left, at the end of the eighteenth century, with a very large group of Methodists, in addition to the Anglicans, in addition to the Presbyterians and the Congregationals, and the Baptists and the Friends, and by the end of the century the Roman Catholics were allowed back in too, so we are beginning to get the kind of picture we live in. We must leave John Wesley and look at one other great man at the end of the century. In 1799 there came a young, dissolute student to Cambridge, Charles Simeon. Hunting, shooting, fishing, he was a cheerful young man, and when he came to Cambridge he came face to face with his own life, and he had a spiritual struggle, and out of it he came to a sense of forgiveness. As he put it: 'I laid my sins on the head of Jesus'. He was shortly ordained to the ministry and at the early age of 23 he went as vicar to Holy Trinity Church, where it has been my privilege to preach. There in the vestry you can see his teapot, his umbrella, and pictures of him. Simeon preached and the church was thronged, and he had a tremendous influence on the students. It was from his congregation that that young man Henry Martyn went out to die in Persia as one of the greatest missionaries there has ever been. Charles Simeon must be put in the great list of heroes of this century.

Consider some of the practical things that came out of this. People sometimes say: 'What is the point of all this Gospel preaching and this hymn singing? What we need is people who get on and make this world a better place. All this hot gospelling and all this ranting it doesn't do anyone any good!' The eighteenth century gives the lie to that. The results of this revival in the eighteenth century were most practical. First, is one that the world wouldn't appreciate but which Christians have appreciated ever since.

THE CENTURY BURST INTO SONG

Think of some of the famous hymns of Isaac Watts: *I'll praise my Maker*; *O God, our help in ages past*; *When I survey the wondrous cross*; *Jesus shall reign where'er the sun*; *Come let us join our cheerful songs*; *Sweet is the work, my God, my King*; *I'm not ashamed to own my Lord*; *Give me the wings of faith to rise*. There was also Philip Doddridge – *Hark the glad sound, the Saviour comes*; *O God of Bethel, by Whose hand*; *O happy day that fixed my choice*. William Cowper: *God moves in a mysterious way*; *There is a fountain filled with blood*; *Jesus, where'er Thy people meet*; *Sometimes a light surprises*. John Newton: *How sweet the name of Jesus sounds*; *Glorious things of Thee are spoken*; *Begone, unbelief* – and the end of that verse: *With Christ in the vessel I can smile at the storm*.

Above all, Charles Wesley, John's brother,

wrote 6,000 hymns and he wrote them for every conceivable occasion. Two of the most wonderful are, firstly, for a young person who leaves home for the first time, he has a hymn for them to sing; another is for a woman in child labour and it is a most beautiful hymn, centring her thoughts on the Lord for her to sing while she is bringing forth her children. Charles would write hymns on horseback and he would arrive at a house and say, 'Don't speak to me. Give me a pen and paper, quick.' And he would write, and out came a hymn. On the first anniversary of his conversion, Peter Bohler, the Moravian German said to Charles Wesley, 'If I had a thousand tongues I would want to sing the praise of Christ', so down it came: *O for a thousand tongues to sing my great Redeemer's praise....* Look at some of the others: *Ye servants of God, your Master proclaim*; *Hark, the herald angels sing*; *Christ the Lord is risen today*; *Rejoice, the Lord is King*; *Lord from whom all blessings flow*; *And can it be that I should gain...?*; *Jesus, Lover of my soul*; *A charge to keep I have*; *Soldiers of Christ, arise*; *O Thou who camest from above*; *Love divine, all loves excelling*; *O for a heart to praise my God.* You will find that more hymns are by Charles Wesley than any other writer, with Isaac Watts a good second. Finally, James Montgomery: *Prayer is the soul's sincere desire*; *Stand up and bless the Lord.* This was a century of song. When people start to get saved they want to sing and there has never been a century like it for hymn singing.

SUNDAY SCHOOLS

Now if I asked you who started Sunday schools I wonder who you would tell me. If you know anything you would probably say 'Robert Raikes' in Gloucester, and I will tell you you are wrong. Sunday schools were started by Hannah Ball in High Wycombe, a Methodist lady who lies buried in Stokenchurch graveyard. Hannah Ball started Sunday schools in a disused furniture factory, and she did so as a result of a correspondence with John Wesley. It was Hannah who suggested to Robert Raikes 'Why don't you do the same?' and the extraordinary thing is that there is a statue of Robert Raikes in Gloucester that says 'Founder of Sunday schools'.

Well, he copied the idea from a woman, but Hannah Ball (if you want to see her grave, it is there on the right hand side of the church as you go in to Stokenchurch graveyard) started Sunday schools and Robert Raikes took it up in 1780 in Gloucester, but she was doing it some years before that.

I picked up a book on *Early Methodist Women* and it had, next door to each other, Frances Pawson and Hannah Ball!

SOCIAL RIGHTEOUSNESS

When people get converted, they put society right. Here are some of the things that followed: Poor relief began; dispensaries distributing free medicine began; orphanages began; schools began; prison reform began. John Howard's work in prison reform goes directly back to the revival of the eighteenth century.

Above all, the outstanding example is William Wilberforce and his fight with slavery. The last letter John Wesley wrote was to Wilberforce, urging him to complete the fight. If ever you go to Kingston-upon-Hull, go to the William Wilberforce Museum. That came out of the revival.

GOOD LITERATURE

Another thing that came out was a tremendous spread of good literature. The Religious Tract Society was a direct result, as was the British and Foreign Bible Society. So were the Commentaries of that great Bible teacher, Thomas Scott.

MISSIONARY SOCIETIES

The final effect I want to mention is that missionary Societies began, and the influence of Britain on the world, for good, spread. There had been some attempts at missionary work before, but it was at the end of the eighteenth century, as the result of the rise in temperature, that it really got going.

In 1792 the Baptist Missionary Society was formed. It was a Baptist that really set it going. A cobbler from Northampton, William Carey, constructed a globe of the world from offcuts of leather and was praying for that world, and particularly for India. It was that Northampton cobbler, converted, encouraged to be a preacher in the Baptist churches of Northamptonshire, who, with a group of others, met one day in Kettering in 1792 and took a collection, a famous collection of £13.2s.6d which was quite a lot in those days, and started the Baptist Missionary Society. A year later they were on their way to India to begin the great missionary work that followed. That was 1792. Three years later the Anglicans, Congregationals and the Presbyterians, not to be outdone, got together and started the London Missionary Society (LMS) which sent out Morrison to China, Livingstone to Africa and many another famous missionary.

In 1796, not to be left behind, the Methodists founded the General Methodist Missionary Society. In 1799, the Anglicans decided to have one of their own and the Church Missionary Society was started, and it was just in this period that the British and Foreign Bible Society was founded.

All of this came at the end of the century and this was the direct result of the Evangelical Revival. Who says that hot gospelling has no results? Who says that the world isn't changed because people get excited about the Lord? The main lesson I draw out of the whole century for you has been that what a man believes will affect his behaviour. Cold intellectualism – bad morals. Hot gospel – and all this follows, and somebody has said that the early Methodists were like a cluster of chaste snowdrops growing on a foul rubbish heap. If you want to understand the Methodists' emphasis on not drinking or gambling you must understand that the tradition goes back to reality in the eighteenth century, and that they had to insist on that to get a man anywhere near the Lord. But they fought, and they cleaned England up.

A French historian said that if you want to understand why the French Revolution and the enthronement of Reason and the anarchy that followed did not spread to England, you must study the life of John Wesley. That is an amazing tribute. God had his answer even when man's cold reason was saying you have to prove anything before you can believe it, and that was killing religion dead, and when you kill religion, you kill morals. When people say 'No God' they will say 'No goodness'.

God raised up men who pointed to revelation, who pointed to God giving us knowledge that science can neither prove nor disprove, and they preached a gospel of supernatural miracle, a *living God* who could step in and change a life and change a society, that neither nature nor human nature was governed by laws but that both were governed by God, and that God could turn both to his eternal purposes. That is a message that we all need to learn. Great men of God got them warmed up again and brought the gospel of Jesus Christ to this land and we still benefit from the effects of that revival.

9

THE NINETEENTH CENTURY (1) 1800 – 1850

By 1800 two things had begun to happen among the people of England. The first was that the great move from the country to the towns had begun. The Industrial Revolution was underway. The steam engine had been invented and this was going to concentrate the people of England in towns and throw them together in living and working conditions that were utterly appalling. It was in the period 1800 to 1850 that Charles Dickens first published *The Pickwick Papers* and if you read that book you will see something of the conditions of the Debtor's Prison and the social life of that era. Britain was beginning to build her 'dark Satanic mills' in 'England's green and pleasant land'.

The second thing that was happening to the people of this period was that they were not only moving into the towns, they were increasing very rapidly in numbers.Bear in mind that in 1800 there were five million people in England. So crowded was England at that time that a clergyman called Malthus was writing *An Essay on the Principle of*

Population, and he was saying, in 1800, 'Britain hasn't enough food to feed all these people. What can we do? We cannot increase the amount of food, so there must be found some way of decreasing the population.' He rejected contraception and said the only thing was for people to marry late and for there to be no social benefits so that large families don't get any help. By the end of that period there were nine million people in Britain.

But things were happening mentally, or perhaps we should say emotionally. We have noted that the eighteenth century began with a movement we call rationalism which was cold; it was of the 'mind'. But the nineteenth century had a reaction to that and the pendulum swung the other way, and the new century began with a change of atmosphere which we call Romanticism. In this movement, three things happened. The first was that people began to be very interested in their feeelings. No longer was the prime interest in 'thought', now the interest was in 'feelings'. If I mention some of the novels that were written in this fifty years, you will get the message. Jane Austen wrote *Pride and Prejudice*. Victor Hugo wrote the *Notre Dame de Paris*. Thackeray wrote *Vanity Fair*. The Bronte sisters were writing up in Haworth in Yorkshire and Charlotte was penning *Jane Eyre* and Emily was writing that incredible story *Wuthering Heights*, and this was to be followed by Trollope's *Barchester Towers* and many another novel. Novels were going back to romance, back to love, back to the feelings that people have for one another, and so the Romantic Movement had begun.

If the first thing was a return to 'feelings', the second thing, that came out of this, was a return to history. People felt that they had thrown overboard too much of the past, that all these new ideas and the French Revolution and the American Declaration of Independence, and all these changes that had occurred, had been too much change of thought, and the heart goes back much further. It is strange: you can change a person's mind fairly quickly, but you can't change their heart very quickly and a person may feel that a change is good but their heart says, 'No I am not going to do it. I'm too fond of the old.' Now because they rediscovered the heart, they rediscovered past history and they began to delve back into the past and to write books about the past, some of them fictional and some of them factual.

Sir Walter Scott was busy writing *Ivanhoe*, Alexandre Dumas was beginning to write *The Three Musketeers* and *The Count of Monte Cristo*, Macaulay was beginning to write *The History of England* and Blackmore was writing *Lorna Doone*. These were all historical books and so we have the great historical romances. Romance felt back into the past. We call it sentiment. Do you like to go back to the house in which you were born? Do you like to go and visit the places you once knew? That is heart feeling. Thought would say there is no point in going back, but your heart says, 'I love to go back and see the old places.' I am incurably sentimental like that. I just love to go back and see places that I once knew, or things connected with the past. The mind will concentrate on the future but the heart concentrates on the past.

Thirdly, this immeasurably brought people's minds back to religion, for religion that is purely of the mind is too cold and hard, but a religion of the heart is going to enrich people. Some of the hymns that were written in this period really touch the heart. *Abide with me, fast falls the eventide.* Now if ever there was a romantic hymn, that is it. If ever a hymn touched deep feelings, that is it, and still to this day it is sung at a football match because deep down people are romantic, deep down they are sentimental, deep down they love feelings and deep down, that kind of hymn touches those feelings.

All this helped religion along and in the first fifty years of the nineteenth century, religion was booming. The various bodies that we have so far brought into the picture through history, the Anglicans, the Methodists, the Baptists, the Congregationals, the Friends and others, were all growing like wildfire, particularly the nonconformists. They soon outstripped the Church of England in growth, and in 1800 5% of the churchgoers were nonconformists, but in 1850 fifty per cent were. The nineteenth century was the great century of the nonconformists and the free churches, particularly the Methodists, and the Baptists coming along behind. This was the great era of the free churches, the Dissenters as they were called in Scotland too. Not only were they growing, but they were dividing, yet, somehow I learn from church history that in a period of growth and expansion churches divide, but talk of unity comes in a period when they are declining.

Now this may sound wrong and I want you to think that through.A living organism grows by division.That is a biological lesson I learned in the laboratory, but the places in the world where the church is growing today are the places where most divisions are occurring and the places where unity is the preoccupation are the places where the church is declining. I am not going to justify divisions on that basis but I just point it out as a fact. This may apply to local churches: the bigger you get, the less you grow; the more you divide, the more you grow. So division is the way the church has expanded over the centuries. But in spite of the divisions that occurred – the Methodist church split into at least three major bodies during this period, the Church of Scotland split into two, and many others split – there was a feeling, 'nevertheless, let us be linked to each other'.

It was during this fifty years that six Baptist churches got together and formed The Baptist Union. Various societies came into being outside the denominations yet cutting right across them. A draper's assistant called George Williams decided to start a new movement to win young men for Christ, and he called it 'The Young Men's Christian

Association' – the YMCA. That has spread all over the world. Mind you, in his day it was a condition that before you could join or even use their facilities that you showed clear evidence of being born again of Christ and the 'C' in the YMCA was very much emphasised, much more so than in modern times.

It was also the great era of Protestant missions. The whole nineteenth century was, but the difference is that in the first half of the century the missionary work was done by the denominations, whereas in the second half of the century it was done by interdenominational missionary societies, particularly following the founding of the China Inland Mission by Hudson Taylor in 1865 which created quite a new pattern of missionary societies.

In 1800–1850, when it was still largely denominational, you had such great missionaries as Henry Martyn who finally decided not to marry a great young lady, a Christian young lady with whom he was deeply in love so that he could go out as a missionary, and he knew he would not be able to take her where he was going and where the Lord had called him. Leaving her behind, he went out to India, translated the New Testament and the Book of Common Prayer into Hindustani, went on into Persia into the most difficult area in the world to mission and died at the age of 31. He was a great Christian if ever there was one.

This was the half century in which a boy was born in Blantyre in Scotland, called David Livingstone, who came to know Christ, and who said, 'I'm going to be a missionary for Christ in China.' Did you know that David Livingstone was intended for China? But God doesn't always let your ideas go through, and God sent David Livingstone out to Robert Moffat, the great missionary in South Africa who was translating the scriptures into tribal languages. Apart from anything else Livingstone got a wife there because he married Robert Moffat's daughter and then, for some fifteen years, opened up the great hinterland on the top of the plateau of Africa, and in opening it up he was able to blaze a trail for missionaries to go in and take the gospel.

This was the era of Alexander Duff, the great Scottish missionary who went out to India in 1829. Samuel Marsden went as a missionary to Australia and New Zealand. That really makes us think, doesn't it? We don't think nowadays of those places as missionary fields and yet they were. This was the day of Robert Morrison going out with the London Missionary Society to China and producing a Chinese dictionary and Bible.

So it was a day not only when the church at home was growing but when the church overseas was growing also.

This was also the great era of hymn writing – Wesley, Watts and others we mentioned earlier, but in fact, that wave of hymn writing spread over into the nineteenth century. If the eighteenth century was noted for the quality of its hymns, the nineteenth was known for their quantity.

In twenty years forty-two hymn books were

published and were used in every denomination bar the Church of England where it was still illegal to sing hymns! One man published a hymn book and went along to his church and had them sing it and found himself 'on the mat' before his bishop. The bishop said, 'Now look, you shouldn't have done this. This is going to upset the boys at the top. Let me have the hymn book and I will publish it in my name and we might get it through.' This is what he did and the good bishop published it in his own name and has had the credit for it ever since. It was Bishop Heber, an Anglican bishop from Calcutta, who finally got hymns on the map for the Church of England, and these are some he wrote: *Brightest and best of the sons of the morning*; *Holy, Holy, Holy, Lord God Almighty* and *The Son of God goes forth to war.*

It was during this time that we had women writing hymns for the first time. Henriette Auber was writing *Our blest Redeemer, e'er He breathed His tender last farewell* and Charlotte Elliott was writing a hymn that has become the most famous hymn of that century I would think: *Just as I am without one plea.*

Marshman, a Baptist missionary who went overseas with William Carey, was translating Indian hymns written by Indian Christians into English and sending them back home, and we were beginning to sing hymns from overseas. One of them was Krishna Pal's hymn *O Thou my soul.*

There were many other hymn writers. A man

called Cotterill wrote *Hail the day that sees Him rise*. Henry Frances Lyte, Vicar of Brixham in Devon was writing *Praise, my soul, the King of heaven* as well as *Abide with me*. John Greenleaf Whittier was writing *Dear Lord and Father of mankind* and *Immortal Love forever full* and *Dear Lord and Master of us all*. He was a farm boy who heard a Scottish peddler singing songs written by Robbie Burns, and it inspired him to have a go and he began to write hymns. He was very much connected with the Quakers and he bewailed the fact that two hundred years of silence had knocked the singing out of Quakers. He wrote his hymns to try and get it back in. He didn't succeed but nevertheless we have his hymns and we rejoice to do so. A man called Conder was writing hymns like *The Lord is King! Lift up thy voice* and many another. J. Anstice, who only lived twenty-eight brief years, wrote *O Lord how happy should we be if we could cast our care on Thee*.

Such hymns help you to worship God and they spring out of this period of history when men were seeking after God's face.

The social welfare that began in the eighteenth century now came to full flood and now I want to tell you some of the appalling conditions under which many people were living. Take first the matter of slavery. William Wilberforce was fighting that because he was a Christian.

The book I would love you to read by William Wilberforce is not about physical slavery at all;

it is about spiritual slavery to sin. It is the best book I have ever read on it. It was because he was interested in setting men's souls free that he was also concerned about their bodies. He fought very hard, and finally in 1807 he persuaded the Prime Minister, William Pitt to promote a bill to abolish slavery in British territories. It took another twenty-six years before it was finally abolished altogether but William Wilberforce lived to see it and he said this: 'Thank God that I should live to see the day in which England is willing to give twenty million pounds sterling for the abolition of slavery.' That is what it cost us. If you can imagine the value of that sum in those days you will understand why the commercial minds of Britain opposed Wilberforce.

The next area of social welfare in which Christians were in the vanguard was that of reforming working conditions. I thought of this when my daughter was ten and when I thought of my little girl I remembered this – that in 1800 children of seven worked from five in the morning until eight at night with half an hour's break at noon. I think of my child at ten and I wouldn't want to see her working in a factory half of that time and neither would you. You owe it to the Christian conscience that your child does not do that.

Think of it, that five year olds were down the coal mines sitting there for twelve hours, opening and shutting the draught doors as the carts were pulled through with coal in! Five year olds! Women and children were crawling on all fours, naked, chained to coal trucks, pulling them backwards and forwards in the darkness until their knees were either torn and bleeding or as hard as camels. This was happening in the 1800s. This was the world of England, in those days. This was the world in which little boys were pushed up the chimneys to sweep them from inside, and you remember Charles Kingsley's protest against that in *Tom and the Water Babies*.

This was the world in which there were no health rules, no inspectors of factories, no laws at all limiting the hours of work for anyone and it was left to a man called Anthony Ashley Cooper, later Lord Shaftesbury, to do something about it. He was a Tory of the Tories. He was a high born, wealthy man, and he went to school at Harrow. One day, coming home from school down Harrow Hill, he saw a pauper's funeral and a group of drunken men were staggering down with a coffin, and they stumbled and the coffin fell and they roared with laughter as it cracked open. They picked up the pieces and went on to the grave. Anthony Ashley Cooper never forgot that, and because he was by this time a believer in the Lord Jesus, he said, 'Lord, I will spend my life for the poor of this land if you will show me how.'

It was many years before that prayer was answered, but it was answered and in 1842 Lord Shaftesbury saw a bill through Parliament, forbidding women and girls to go down coal mines and forbidding boys under thirteen to work down there. A few years later, he saw the famous Ten Hour Bill in which factory work was limited to ten hours, in which no child under nine could be employed and in which ten hours was the maximum work. This was Lord Shaftesbury, a Christian, and on the top of every sheet of notepaper he ever wrote on were these words: 'Even so, come, Lord Jesus!' and it was the Second Coming of our Lord that inspired him to do that. These were the days of the prison reform with which the names of Elizabeth Fry and John Howard will be forever associated and these were the days of the beginning of widespread education in this land. Bear in mind that in 1800 your children and mine would hardly have stood a chance of any schooling. You would need to be very wealthy. You would need to be fairly high born to get that education, but during this fifty years Christians (mark that – Christians) saw the danger of illiteracy and they fought hard.

In 1811, the Anglicans formed the National Society for Education, and three years later, not to be outdone, the nonconformists started the British and Foreign School Society, and the schools of the land began.

They believed in those days that schools should not be in the hands of the state but in the hands of the church and the schools were started that way. It was not until 1870 that the state took them over and asked the churches to give up their schools which the Free churches did entirely and the Church of England did partly and the Roman Catholic church did not do at all. Prior to that you will find it was the Christians who brought education to the ordinary boy and girl in England. Scotland, of course, had been way ahead as they usually have been in matters of education, and John Knox had already demanded a school and a church in each parish.

Christians were engaged in stopping the opium trade. Christians were engaged in stopping flogging in the Forces. The Christian conscience was busy with social reforms like these.

What was happening to the Church of England during this fifty years? Stirring things were happening which changed the Church of England and still affected it in the twentieth century. Something happened in 1830 which wrecked the attempt to unite the Anglicans and the Methodists in 1967, such was the importance of the period.

We finished the story last time with the state of play within the Church of England around 1800 like this: there were three groups, low, broad and high, or to give you their proper names: evangelical, latitudinarian and catholic. The low were evangelical and stuck to the scriptures and the 39 Articles. The 'broad' were sitting loose to all beliefs and were beginning to preach all kinds of human philosophy and opinions. The 'high' were seeking to recover the catholic practices which marked the church before the days of the Reformation.

The low party or evangelicals were strong in patches. Like the 'curate's egg' it was good in parts, and one of those good parts was Cambridge, where the saintly Charles Simeon was still preaching and drawing crowds to Holy Trinity church. The evangelical Anglicans were growing but were not the majority by any manner of means. Within those patches there were two groups, one of which has now died out and one of which still meets, which were going to have a profound influence. One was a group of laymen and the other was a group of clergy. The group of laymen were known as the Clapham Sect because they met in Clapham. To that group belonged William Wilberforce, John Thornton, who became the first treasurer at the British and Foreign Bible Society, Zachary Macaulay and many another famous Englishman.

They met first as a housegroup for prayer and Bible study, and out of that they developed a social conscience, and the Clapham Sect had a profound influence on our nation's life because they worked through Parliament to remove the evils of our society.

The other group from the Church of England at the evangelical end were called the Islington Clerical Conference. They have continued to meet every year since the first half of the nineteenth century. They seek to get the Church of England onto evangelical lines.

Now we come to the broad church, which was then perhaps the majority group and it was in a bad way. Such religion was dead, it had no 'go' in it because there was no foundation of real belief. It was worldly and cold. It was 'religion' rather than Christianity, and sooner or later, people who are in that get so dissatisfied with it that they do something about it, and in 1827 a group of men did something about it, not in England but in Dublin – Anthony Norris Groves, a retired missionary, John Parnell, later Lord Congleton, J. G. Bellett, a lawyer, Dr Cronin, W. F. Hutchinson, and a man who was, at the beginning, an Anglican curate, called John Nelson Darby. From that group has come the movement which we know as the Brethren. It is very important and interesting to note that they came out of a dead Anglican situation, for this explains both their affinities with the Church of England and their aversion to it, and it explains a very great deal of what has happened ever since. They came out of that dead background of broad Anglicanism which had nothing real to offer them by way of salvation, and they got together and decided to seek to go right back to the New Testament and start all over again, and seek to have worship according to the New Testament pattern. For this reason they abolished the ministry and simply met together and asked the Lord to minister to them through each other. They placed tremendous emphasis, and this has been their strength, on Bible knowledge. Of all the denominations, I would say the Brethren know their Bibles better than any other. It is also quite fair to add that they know their interpretation of them better than any other, as well as the scriptures themselves, and I know that remark will be taken in good part. They met together, and with this emphasis on the Bible there went an emphasis on the near return of our Lord Jesus Christ, which is always a healthy motive in Christian living, and with that also there went a tremendous emphasis on the priesthood of all believers. Those who joined the group who had been Anglicans cut adrift from clericalism and 'churchianity' and became simply brethren, calling themselves by the name which Christians used in the New Testament.

Now the movement spread, or spontaneously sprang up in many other parts. It spread from Dublin to Plymouth, and in Plymouth was the first real group of Brethren in this country and that is why many people, to their annoyance, call them the Plymouth Brethren. (It is not because they found Plymouth Sound, as some suggested.)

Now the leader there, of course, was a man called B.W. Newton and he was, after some years of good ministry, accused of being a heretic and preaching false doctrine, and a split occurred. Some of those who had been with him in Plymouth left and went over to Bristol where a chapel had developed a kind of worship and churchmanship very close to theirs. It was called Bethesda Chapel. There in Bethesda Chapel were two men leading a congregation on Brethren lines. One was George Muller, a man with tremendous faith; he saw a million pounds flow in to support an orphanage which lived on in Bristol (one of the few orphanages that never advertised its needs). Henry Craik and George Muller gathered up some of the fragments of the split that occurred over Newton. J.N. Darby was not so happy about it and broadly speaking Darby became the leader of the exclusive brethren, and George Muller and Henry Craik became the pioneers of the open brethren. The difference between them was fairly simple: the open brethren would have relationships with Christians outside themselves; the exclusive brethren would not. Another great difference was that the open brethren were entirely independent churches governing their own affairs but the exclusive brethren were more centrally organised from the top which, by the way, explains why if you get a good man at the top this has a good influence all through, but if you get the wrong man it immediately influences every part of the movement.

From being a Chaplain in the Royal Air Force, it always thrilled my heart to see somebody registered on a card as 'Brethren'. They had to register in the Forces as 'Plymouth Brethren', for some reason. That was the only official title Her Majesty would recognise. I found that if I saw that on a card, I could be sure I was going to get a Christian into the Forces and that he would be a grand worker, but if I saw other things I would get some good young men and some completely nominal. I say this, because it means, and I give this tribute, that the Brethren have exerted an influence in Christian circles out of all proportion to their numbers, but in direct proportion to their quality. Among the main lacks one has noticed is a lack of social conscience and social activity.

The social reforms and removal of evils in the nineteenth century was largely left to the evangelical Anglicans to see through, and the Clapham Sect that I have mentioned.

We now turn our attention to the high church party. The low church party in the Church of England had its Clapham Sect for laymen and its Islington Clerical Conference for ministers. The broad church was dead, worldly and cold and in reaction to that, the Christian Brethren arose as a separate party. But the high church in 1830 received a tremendous boost – and it all started in Oxford. It is called the Oxford Movement.

It happened like this. In 1828 the obnoxious Test Act was repealed. That law had forbidden Roman Catholics and nonconformists to be Members of Parliament. So from 1828 a nonconformist or Roman Catholic could become a Member of Parliament in England. Bear in mind that the Parliament of England controlled the Church of England, and suddenly Anglican clergy woke up to the fact that nonconformists and Roman Catholics were going to control their church. This alarmed a group of churchmen in Oxford who saw a red light in this. These churchmen in Oxford were led by John Henry Newman, Richard Hurrell Froude, Edward Pusey, John Keble and F.W. Faber. They said, 'We must put the church right now and put it back to what it was and put it back in God's hands and out of men's hands.' This was their basic aim. They said, 'We must treat the church as a divine thing and not a human thing, not a thing for Members of Parliament to push around but a thing for God to direct. How can we do it?' and because they were right in this Romantic Movement they said, 'We will do it by going back to what we were'.

Instead of going back to the New Testament as the Brethren tried to do, they looked back to the Middle Ages and the Latin and Greek fathers. So they began to teach the most extraordinary things and they published them in a series of little Tracts, about 120 of them altogether, so that some refer to this as the Tractarian movement. Here are some of the things they taught: that the only valid ministers are those who have been ordained by bishops; that the only valid bishops are those who can claim a succession that goes right back 2000 years to Christ; that when a baby is baptised it is born again of the Spirit and becomes a Christian; that a priest actually makes the bread and wine into Christ's body and blood. John Henry Newman wrote this in one of his tracts and it is where they really came unstuck: they said it is perfectly alright for a clergyman of the Church of England to say that he believes the 39 Articles and to reserve the right to give them his own meaning.

Now this was a blow at the heart of the Church of England and such an uproar was raised over this that John Henry Newman went off and joined the Roman Catholic church and became a Cardinal in it, and many of the other Tractarians from Oxford did the same. The tragedy is that they hadn't done this in the first place, because the effect of their work was that it changed the Church of England radically – instead of their work collapsing when they went and joined Rome, the church that says 'We've got bishops that go all the way back.'

Here is a paragraph from Bishop Knox, writing in 1933, 'Probably even Newman or Pusey would be astounded if they could visit the scenes of their old labours and could see bishops mitred and vested in copes and chasubles, clergy and churches so ornamented as to be indistinguishable from those of Rome, images of the virgin Mary with lights burning before them, pyxes, monstrances and like evidences of worship of the Host, and could hear the Mass offered in Anglican churches for the living and the dead.' This movement which sought to do good brought Roman practice back in to the Church of England, and you can see the effect of this movement in most parish churches in this land.

All that is critical, and I think it was the most tragic thing that happened to the Church of England since the Reformation. In the following century it was to wreck the conversations with Methodism, because what brought those conversations to a grinding halt was the Anglo-Catholics, who insisted that any united church must have a succession of bishops that goes back to the Middle Ages and through the Middle Ages.

Having said that, may I say that they did a lot

of good too. They produced hymns that show a deep piety. And because of their seriousness over religion, because of their desire that the church should be a divine thing and because of their putting Christ in the centre of their thinking, I find myself with far more in common with the high Anglican than I do with the broad, and I think evangelical Anglicans would tell you the same thing.

If only we could drop the Roman side of it, the bishops side of it and all the vestments and all the ritual and liturgy side of it. I don't think that is needed to make the church what it ought to be, but the centrality of Christ is needed.

Here are a few of the hymns these men wrote. John Keble: *Blest are the pure in heart*; *New every morning is the love.* John Henry Newman: *Praise to the Holiest in the height*; *Lead, kindly light, amidst the encircling gloom.* (I remember a couple asking if they could have that one at their wedding and I thought, 'What a hymn to choose'!) Faber wrote: *My God, how wonderful Thou art*; *There's a wideness in God's mercy.* Pusey wrote: *Lord of our life and God of our salvation.* Others wrote: *Good Christian men, rejoice*; *Jerusalem the golden*; *O happy band of pilgrims*; *See amid the winter's snow*; *Jesus, the very thought of Thee*; *When morning gilds the skies.*

They gave us some of our very best hymns. In an Anglo-Catholic hymn you will always have the sense that God is holy, that the church is to be holy. The tragedy is that this was mixed up with so much 'return' – romantic return to the Middle Ages' ritual and liturgy – and has disguised this deep piety which was at the heart of it.

We finish at the end of 1850 and in the next chapter I want to look at the greatest fifty years from an evangelical point of view.

Two men were busy writing in 1850 and they were going to be the greatest hindering factor to the Christian faith in the next hundred years. One of them was going to sweep Christianity almost off the face of a third of the world. He was a German Jew, writing in the British Museum. His name? Karl Marx, who was writing his book *Das Kapital*. He had already published the *Communist Manifesto* some years earlier but now he sat writing a book that was to change the course of history. Charles Darwin, after a voyage on *The Beagle* round the South Sea Islands, was writing *On the Origin of Species*. *Das Kapital* and *On the Origin of Species* were going to be used, almost against their authors' knowledge, and certainly against Darwin's will and desire, to attack the Christian faith as it had never been attacked before in history. It is as if heaven was getting ready for this attack; as if God the Holy Spirit knew it was coming and decided, in 1859, to pour out on England such a revival, such a Holy Spirit movement, such a changing of society and of men and women, such a sweeping of thousands into the kingdom of God, as would be able to bring the church through that next fifty years.

Christ was going to keep his church. Christ was

going to build his church. He didn't tell us to, he said, 'I will build my church'. As I study the history of the church I can see Jesus Christ standing in the shadows, sending his Holy Spirit when it is needed, to strengthen his people, to bring them through, and the one society that will never disappear from this world of ours is the church of Jesus Christ. It won't disappear until he comes again, and then the complete church will reign with him in glory. Praise his name.

10

THE NINETEENTH CENTURY (2) 1850 – 1900

1850 to 1900 was the age of women. It was reigned over by a woman who gave her name to the age – The Victorian Age. The period we are going to consider now is really the reign of Queen Victoria. It was also the period of Florence Nightingale and many another famous woman.

It was a churchgoing era. On a certain Sunday in 1851 a census was taken of churchgoing in England and 40% of the population of England was in church on that Sunday, an ordinary Sunday in the month of February. Most of us realise that in the Victorian age far more people worshipped God than do today. We owe a great deal to that age. A minister said to me (he had been in the Church of England and is now a Baptist minister) – 'When I made the change, I moved from the Middle Ages to the Victorian era!' I think I can understand what he meant. He moved out of a denomination whose buildings were largely medieval or modelled on that style to a chapel or a denomination with chapels that were largely Victorian. In the 1960s I observed that Baptist hymns were Victorian, our buildings were Victorian and I am afraid, sometimes, our outlook was Victorian. Much of that was to change in the late twentieth century, but I think we could have been excused for this a little, because the Victorian age was undoubtedly the greatest age in this country for the gospel. I want to describe why.

This was the age in which Britain was building an empire on which 'the sun would never set'. It all sounds a little strange to us today. This was the day when Britain could perhaps be described as 'Influence No.1' in the world, a day when we counted. This was the day when we influenced the world for good in many ways because the Holy Spirit was at work in our land.

Now I want to divide what I have to say into two parts: 'What the Holy Spirit did during these fifty years' and, 'What the devil did during these fifty years' – and the second is one of the saddest parts of the story that I have been trying to unfold for you.

First of all let us look at the happy things, and I want to ask what the Holy Spirit did in the 1850s, the 1860s, the 70s, the 80s, then the 90s, and in every decade there was some outstanding work of the Holy Spirit, for which we are still grateful to God and from which we still enjoy the benefits.

To start with the 1850s, in 1857 revival broke out. The Holy Spirit swept in power and swept two million people into the church in two years. It did not break out in England. It broke out in America in 1857 and within a few years a million people in America had been converted and joined the church. From America the revival spread as a prairie fire does, to Ulster in Northern Ireland and from Ulster it spread to England, and by 1859, two years after it had started in America, England was enjoying revival. In England, as in America, a million people were added to the body of Christ in a very few years. It is a thrilling story and if you want to read about it, read the book by J. Edwin Orr on *The Evangelical Awakening*. He got his doctorate for writing that up incidentally, and it is a wonderful account of God's Holy Spirit moving in revival.

Now the significance of this revival was this: for the first time America was leading England spiritually. This has been a pattern since. For the previous 100 or 150 years, England took the initiative and sent the gospel to America. It was from England that life went across the Atlantic. Since 1857 it has been the other direction. This is sometimes resented in this country. We say, 'Why don't they stay and convert the hoodlums of New York and Chicago? Why send American evangelists over here?' Funnily enough, the British didn't talk like that when they were sending evangelists over there. We are so 'one directional' in our thinking that we can't bear to be on the receiving end, but this is how it had come and during the last hundred years America has, again and again, stimulated our spiritual life. In the previous hundred we had stimulated theirs.

During the beginning of the revival, in 1857, a twenty year old young businessman, Dwight L. Moody, was converted. Although he continued in his business for some years, he finally decided the Lord would have him go all out to preach the gospel. Finding a man who could sing called Ira D. Sankey, Moody and Sankey set off on their travels and I would say that, in spite of the great things we have seen in this century, there has never been such a great evangelist from America as Dwight L. Moody in his day. The results of his campaigns are with us still.

Now the result of that revival in the 1850s was that in the 1860s we had a crop of great men who owed their spiritual life to the previous decade, and who changed the course of Christian history. I just want to pick out three of them to give you an idea of the quality of those who had come from that revival.

First, Dr Thomas Barnardo was a medical man, training to go out as a missionary to China, but he never got farther than London. Why? Because one night he found a boy and said, 'Why aren't you at home?' and the boy said, 'I have no home to go to.'

Dr Barnardo was shocked and said, 'But surely you have some home?'

The boy replied, 'No I haven't. Nor have any of us.'

'Any of you? How many are there of you?'
'Hundreds!'

'Show me' – and the little urchin from the East End of London took Dr Barnardo round the places, the warehouses, and lifted the tarpaulins and showed him the boys, and Dr Barnardo realised that God would have him stay in London and not go to China, and meet the needs of those boys. I shouldn't think there is any reader from the British Isles who doesn't know the name of Dr Barnardo or hasn't heard of the homes he started for those boys, the motto of which was this: *No destitute child ever refused admission* – or, in popular language: the 'ever open door'.

Another man who was raised up by God in the 1860s as the result of that revival in the 1850s was William Booth who, with his wife Catherine, started something that is still with us until this day: The Salvation Army. William Booth was a Methodist minister, but by this time Methodism had got too respectable and was not winning souls as it used to do, and he was so quickened by the revival that he went out into the streets and he got folk converted. He preached. He would use any method. He would bang a drum, blow a trumpet, do anything to get through to people and get them won for the Lord. But this was not very acceptable to his superiors in the denomination and there came a memorable Conference of Methodism when William Booth was asked to stop this and not do so much unconventional evangelism. As he stood before them and wavered, a female voice from the gallery shouted *'Never, William! Never!'* and

Catherine really started the Salvation Army at that moment.

They plunged into the East End of London and found indescribable need. About that time, a great explorer, whose name you know, came back from Africa and published *In Darkest Africa*.

A year later, William Booth published *In Darkest England – and the Way Out*, in which he uncovered the economic, social and moral needs of London. He gathered around him a group of men and women and finally, in the 1870s he said, 'We must be an army for Christ', and he organised this group as an army, with uniforms, with bands, with orders from above, with a rigid discipline, and he fought his battles.

One of the great battles that I love to hear of is the battle for open air meetings. There were many local areas that didn't like open air meetings and one of them was the rather exclusive resort on the south coast called Eastbourne. They didn't like religion on the streets and so they had a bye-law against it and anybody who did it would be taken to the police station. So the local group of soldiers of the Salvation Army had their open air meeting and were taken to the police station. William Booth sent out an order to every available soldier all over England: '*Come to Eastbourne and start an open air meeting!*' Every train that came into Eastbourne disgorged more soldiers and they had their meetings. The police station was full, they commandeered a local school, they arrested more and they filled that, but he won his battle and Eastbourne finally capitulated to the invasion of this Army. So then he could go everywhere else and say, 'Eastbourne doesn't mind open air meetings!' – and the battle was won. They suffered violence, they were mocked, they were misunderstood, but they went ahead.

One thing William Booth refused to do, which may or may not have been a mistake, I don't know, was that he refused to be a church, and that is why, basically, he refused either to baptise or to have the Lord's Supper, because his whole aim was to take people, get them into Christ and put them in a church and finish with them then and let the church go on. Had that worked out it would have been great, but of course it didn't work out. The churches of his day, as a century before with the converts of the Methodists, would not receive them and so he had to provide fellowship for them. So to this day they have remained separately in their corps., still without baptism and the Lord's supper. It is interesting that I had a chat with General Coutts and he told me that many officers feel that they should have these things and that they were missing them.

They soon plunged into social activities and welfare work and I would say that the outsider now knows them better for their social work than for their spiritual, but I believe that in the mid-twentieth century there came a new lease of life and a new approach to the problems and a desire to change methods. God is going to use the Salvation

Army again in the future, in a great way.

The third man we will look at is Hudson Taylor. We recall again that all these great figures were thrown up by the revival of the 1850s and they appeared on the front of the stage in the 1860s and the 1870s. The date to remember is 1865. I hardly dare to begin to give you anything of the life of this Yorkshire lad, of his spiritual crisis on the shores of a southern coast resort as he battled with God, and as God broke him and won the battle; of this man who was so terribly troubled by the millions dying in China, and who went out because of that burden.

Suffice to say that out of his work came the China Inland Mission which became the Overseas Missionary Fellowship.

That mission changed the pattern of missionary work, quite decisively, for a large part of the outreach into other lands. Two differences between his approach to missionary work and the approach of all the societies beforehand have affected everyone's thinking since. On the one hand, he did something which was much broader than previous societies. On the other hand, he did something which was much narrower. On the broader scale, he was prepared to have missionaries from any denomination in his mission. Prior to that, you had the Baptist Missionary Society, the Methodist Missionary Society, the London Missionary Society, the Church (or Church of England) Missionary Society – denominational societies. Now for the first time was a new mission that was interdenominational and broader in its basis.

The other thing he did which was so outstanding was much narrower, and it is a thing that has caused a great deal of discussion and debate since, and it concerned finance and recruits. Prior to that, the need for money and recruits was always shared with the church at large and the whole church was expected to have the faith for the money and the men so that the Baptist Society in India would send home and say to the whole church, 'This is our need for money, for men, for anything else', and the church, as the whole family of God, would get under the burden and pray and seek to find what was needed.

But from the start of the CIM onwards, it was decided that it was wrong to do this, that it was a breach of faith to do anything other than let the Lord know, and the needs for men and money were kept within the mission and not shared with the church. In other words, the family that had to exercise the faith was now limited to those who were actually on the field or in the mission. In this sense, they were narrower.

I would say it is right for some to do one thing and for some to do another, as the Lord guides, but for these two principles and particularly the second, Hudson Taylor became nicknamed a 'faith missioner', and the term 'faith mission' came in at this point. I think it is a great pity it came in. It was a nickname. He didn't choose it and others chose it for him, but it implied that all the other societies before him were not faith missions. I would say that faith was being exercised in a different way and they were led in one way and other societies were led in another.

From the CIM has come a whole host of other Missionary Societies in the period we are considering. The Africa Inland Mission, Regions Beyond Missionary Union and a host of others could be mentioned. All were interdenominational but limited their mention of need to the mission and didn't feel free to mention the needs, particularly of money, to the church at large. That is the significance of Hudson Taylor and it changed missionary thinking from 1865 onwards.

Britain, during this period, was still leading the world in missionary effort but was rapidly being overtaken by the Americans, as we note elsewhere.

In the 1870s I detect a movement for the deepening of spiritual life in this land. It started in 1870 in Mildmay, London, where the vicar, William Pennefeather, built a large hall to seat 2,500 people and he opened that hall for meetings to make better Christians of people. Two years later, he said to Mr Moody, 'Will you come over and preach for us?' and this was the point at which Moody and Sankey came in to Britain.

They came in 1873 and in that year they preached to two and a half million people in London alone. That was without closed-circuit television and without modern publicity agents and without any of the aids to large meetings that we have today.

They toured Ireland, England, Scotland and wherever they went, rich and poor, educated and illiterate, flocked to hear this American evangelist, and Sankey's hymns were still being used in the twentieth century. The music, I think, contributed as much as the preaching perhaps. The two were a perfect team.

Now one of the results was that when Moody went back to the United States, a group began to meet together to seek the Spirit-filled life, and among them was the Vicar of Keswick, the Rev. T. D. Harford-Battersby, and a Quaker, Robert Wilson. They met together as a small group to be filled with the Spirit, and out of that, the vicar of Keswick said, 'Why not have a Convention in Keswick, in the Lake District to help people to do just this?' – and in 1875 the first Keswick Convention was held. Now you can go all over the world and you will find this name. You can go to New Zealand and you can go to the Keswick Convention. You can go to America and you can go to the Keswick Convention.

In 1876, the next year, a group of Christian students got together in Cambridge and started what they called the Cambridge Inter-Collegiate Christian Union, colloquially known as CICCU, and if you have been to Cambridge you will know what CICCU stands for and is. In 1879, OICCU (otherwise known as the Oxford Inter-Collegiate Christian Union) began and all over England Christian Unions sprang up and ultimately became linked in what was then called the SCM – Student Christian Movement. So 'Christian Unions' and SCM were originally one, and the Christian Unions met in the SCM.

In the 1880s the greatest thing that happened was that, for the first time in over two hundred years, there was a new translation of the Bible, but alas, it never proved popular and never really caught on. It was called The Revised Version of 1880. Many years ago I was fascinated to see C.T. Studd's Bible – or one of them. He had a new one every year because he used them up at that rate. It was full of his notes and lines and comments, and he had used the Revised Version of 1880. But other things were happening in 1880 which concerned C. T. Studd. In 1882 Moody went to Cambridge and people said: 'A revivalist at Cambridge, in an intellectual atmosphere? Never! It will be a flop'. But D. L. Moody came and tremendous things happened in that university among the intellectuals who were saying, by that time, Christianity is out-of-date, scientists have proved it wrong. As a result, two years later, seven famous students and sportsmen set off for China, among them the test cricketer Studd, so what followed from his work, including the Worldwide Evangelisation Crusade with 1,100 missionaries and its local headquarters at Bulstrode Park, came out of Moody's visit to Cambridge.

Now something was happening in America among the students at this time, in Princeton University. In 1886, a student called Robert Wilder gathered another group of students around him and said, 'Let's pray for a thousand students to go overseas as missionaries, to preach the gospel.' Very soon they had hundreds of students offering to go as missionaries and they called themselves the Student Volunteer Movement. This idea spread through the student world and at a meeting in Edinburgh in the next decade, in 1892, the Student Volunteer Movement was formally inaugurated with the motto above it 'The evangelisation of the world in this generation'. This was their object and very soon a thousand students were in the field. In twenty-five years, nine thousand students went overseas to preach the gospel. One of the leaders of this movement was a great man called John R. Mott. You may have heard that name, but he was converted, humanly speaking, by the brother of C.T. Studd. In 1895, the Christian Endeavour, which had started as a small meeting in a Congregational church in London, became the World Christian Endeavour Union, and became another worldwide sweep of Christian activity.

Now that is the kind of thing the Holy Spirit was doing in this half century, and as you would imagine, out of this ferment of spiritual life there came hymns and preachers.

Some of the greatest preachers came in this period. Charles Haddon Spurgeon was one, Keir Hardie, the founder of the Independent Labour Party, was another great evangelist, and in the original Labour Party there were many Christians.

Hugh Price Hughes, F. W. Robertson of Brighton and many another great preacher, may be just names to you, if that; but the hymns survived. Torrey and Alexander were two more who came over from the States – Torrey, the preacher, and Alexander, the singer.

Here are some of the hymns that came out of this period – Frances J. van Alstyne, that blind girl, wrote *To God be the glory*; *Fill Thou my life*; *Praise Him, Praise Him, Jesus our blessed Redeemer, Jesus is tenderly calling*; *Blessed assurance Jesus is mine*; *Rescue the perishing*. Frances Ridley Havergal – *Master, speak Thy servant heareth*; *Lord, speak to me that I may speak*; *Take my life and let it be*; *Who is on the Lord's side?* Christina Rossetti – *In the bleak midwinter*; *None other Lamb*. Mrs C.F. Alexander – *Once in royal David's city*; *There is a green hill far away*; *All things bright and beautiful*. Harriet Beecher Stowe – *Still, still with Thee*. Anna Letitia Waring – *In heavenly love abiding*; *My heart is resting, O my God*. Arabella Catherine Hankey – *I love to tell the story*.

All this even inspired the Prime Minister to have a go, and William Ewart Gladstone was writing hymns. When you've got an English Prime Minister, between cabinet meetings, writing hymns, you've really got something. It was a great burst of hymn singing.

It looked as if the church was going to sweep into the twentieth century and make the world Christian in a very short time, and in 1900 many Christians believed the world would be 'Christian' by about 1930 at the latest. They came into the twentieth century believing the Millennium was almost here. Such had been the flow of spiritual life from 1857 to 1900 that they thought nothing could stop the gospel now.

Alas! The devil was very busy and during these fifty years the devil had done five things which were going to bring the gospel almost to a standstill in some parts of the world and were going to help to kill the church in England to a remarkable degree. The devil was not going to sit and let this happen without putting up a fight. (His days are numbered and I believe that he has lost the battle.)

From the very area of America where the revival had started, he was raising up false cults who would come with a Bible in their hands and claim to be Christians. From the eastern shores of America, this is what he had planned. There were the Mormons, in 1830, with Joseph Smith's fantastic tales about finding a golden book which, unfortunately, the angel took away from him so he couldn't produce it later. There were the Seventh Day Adventists in 1831, the Spiritists in 1848, Christian Science in 1876 and the Jehovah's Witnesses in 1881.

Nearly all these cults and sects started on the Atlantic seaboard of America, and often at the heart of them was a perverted view of the return of Christ. You and I have to answer our door to brethren from over the Atlantic who are seeking to purvey this perverted Christianity. They vary, and some are much nearer to the Christian position than others. The Seventh Day Adventists are very much nearer than the Jehovah's Witnesses. Jehovah's Witnesses are perhaps the biggest cult that started up in this period.

The fundamental thing on which many of them fall down is this: they do not believe that Jesus is God. Yet they hold a Bible in their hands and can pick texts out of it to bamboozle you, and think that they are the only ones who know the Bible. The only defence against that kind of thing is a person who knows their Bible better. Frankly, most of their converts are made from churchgoers who have not had Bible teaching in their church. It is as simple as that.

That was the devil's first fighting back. You can find Jehovah's Witnesses today in parts of the world where you cannot find missionaries. They are among the most zealous and ardent people you will ever come across. Indeed, if I go to a door in a long raincoat and carry a briefcase I will certainly be thought to be one of them and will have to explain straight away. This is the measure of the devil's mobilisation of the forces at his disposal and it is a tragedy that such zeal is misguided.

Now the second thing the devil did during this fifty years was to make the Roman church more Roman than ever and harden it in certain things. In the early part of the period, the Pope revived the Jesuits, which was a master stroke and they established themselves in many lands. In 1850 the Pope re-established the English hierarchy and said, 'Now we can pick up where England left off in the reign of Henry VIII'. In 1854 the Jesuits persuaded the Pope to start saying things about Mary that were not in the Bible. He said that Mary was born without sin. That is what is meant by the 'immaculate conception' of the Virgin Mary. For centuries the Roman church believed that it was infallible, but nobody knew where the infallibility lay. In 1870 the Pope called together the first Vatican Council since the Council of Trent hundreds of years earlier and almost shocked them all by announcing that the infallibility of the church resides in the Pope. It was only in 1870 that the Pope was declared to be infallible when he sits on his 'throne', his 'cathedra' and speaks *ex cathedra* – from his seat – about what we are to believe or how we are to behave.

The funny thing is that not until 1950 was that prerogative ever exercised! The Pope said, 'I can speak infallibly', but he never did until 1950 when he proclaimed the bodily assumption of the Virgin Mary, namely, that she went to heaven and ascended with her body. Now it is strange that they hadn't used that teaching, and the reason why they didn't was because not all Roman Catholics agreed with it – but he had said it and this hardened Rome and gave her a stronger desire than ever to bring everybody under the authority of an infallible Papacy. That was a stroke of Satan!

The third stroke of Satan was in the scientific

realm. Now I must be careful here. I am not against science. I spent as many years at the university studying science as I did theology. In 1859, Charles Darwin, who had been destined for the ministry, and was the grandson of Josiah Wedgwood, the pottery man, and grandson of the man who first thought of evolution, Erasmus Darwin, who wrote about it many, many years before (Charles Darwin was not original here, he was simply producing his grandfather's scheme and ideas) published *On the Origin of Species*. Just before he published it, he found out that a man called Alfred Russel Wallace had published an essay on exactly the same thing and had reached the same conclusions, and Charles Darwin decided to withdraw his book and let Wallace get all the credit. However, Wallace was a very humble man and said, 'No, let your book go out. It says the same thing.' I would like to guarantee most people today do not know the name of Alfred Russel Wallace, but everyone knows the name of Charles Darwin. He got the credit for it because his book went out.

In this book he did not state that 'men come from monkeys'. If you've got the idea that Charles Darwin said that, then drop it, because he never did say that. His idea was that monkeys and men have come from something else, in common. Now that is a very definite thing and it is very important to understand what he did say. It was a theory, a guess and it still is. There is still utterly inadequate evidence to make this a scientific fact.

The tragedy is that it is taught to our children as proven fact when it is still an interesting hypothesis and nowhere near proved. But what really happened was this. Here is how Darwin finishes: *'I see no good reason why the views given in this volume should shock the religious feelings of anyone. There is grandeur in this view of life with its several powers, having been originally breathed by the Creator into a few forms or into one.'* In other words, he believed in a Creator and Charles Darwin was shattered when people all over the country said, 'Charles Darwin proves there is no Creator.' He said, *'I never proved that and I never said that. I simply said that 'This was how the Creator made us. I do not rule out the Creator.'* But people began to say, *'Well, if a Creator wasn't needed to make the various species, why is the Creator needed at all. It all made itself'* – and the view that the world created itself came sweeping in on us.

Alas, there were misunderstandings on both sides. This was seen as a direct contradiction of the book of Genesis and the battle started, which is most unfortunate. Neither side really understood what the other was saying. People said, 'Evolution is a proved fact' when it wasn't, and people assumed the Bible said things it didn't say. The result was there was a complete impasse. Only a few great Christians like Henry Drummond in Scotland tried to come to some kind of understanding that truth in science and truth in scripture cannot contradict each other because God is truth and he made both, the world that science investigates and the scripture that we read.

Well, it is a battle that, I am afraid, caused thousands of people to leave the church. They believed that you couldn't believe in science and in scripture. Thank God we have grown up a bit from those days and realised that there is much more to be said on this.

So the third area of attack was that the devil certainly got instilled into people's minds that you couldn't go on believing the scripture without denying science or that you couldn't believe science without denying the scripture. That is a false antithesis. We do not have to choose between two truths. Truth is one and whatever science proves (and not just guesses or theorises) must line up with what God has said, because God is truth.

The fourth thing the devil did was to spread atheistic and agnostic ideas. He did this through people like Thomas Carlyle who, when he became an agnostic, was training for the Church of Scotland ministry. He did it through such people as Mary Ann Evans, better known for her pen-name of George Eliot, author of *Mill on the Floss*. He did it through John Stuart Mill, and the scepticism at the heart of his philosophy. He did it through Herbert Spencer, an agnostic. He did it through the Germans particularly through men like Schopenhauer and through men like Feurbach, who said that 'man has made God in *his* image and God is simply a dream.' He did it through people like Nietzsche, who said that 'the will to power is the only thing that drives men and that Jews and Christians have a slave mentality and a slave morality.' It was on Nietzsche's ideas that Hitler came to power and built his life.

So many of these people came from Christian stock. Robert Green Ingersoll deliberately devoted his life to travelling around England and giving lectures on atheism, and in those days if you wanted to be very naughty you went to one. One day a great Christian saw Ingersoll standing at a bus stop in the rain. He went up to him and said, 'Mr Ingersoll, I have just seen a most terrible thing done.' Ingersoll said, 'What is that?' He said, 'I just saw an old lady staggering across the road leaning heavily on a stick and some young man rushed out and pulled the stick from under her and she fell and he left her floundering in the mud.' Mr Ingersoll said, 'Where is he? Who did this dreadful thing?' and the Christian said, 'It was you. You are travelling around this country, knocking away the faith on which people have depended and you leave them floundering with nothing in its place.' It was a fitting rebuke but the devil was spreading these ideas.

One man who wrote in this period and published his book in 1867, whose avowed atheism was to sweep religion out of a third of the world at one stage in the twentieth century, was Karl Marx – through his book *Das Kapital*. The sentence in the book which he borrowed from Charles Kingsley, author of *Tom and the Water Babies,* was 'Religion is the opiate of the people', and he said that when capitalism went, religion must go too. That book became one of the devil's major weapons in bringing millions of people under atheist teaching.

The final weapon that the devil had and the most subtle of all, and the one with which he won the major battle in the twentieth century, was this – people began to treat the Bible in the wrong way, and it is significant that the name that was given to this treatment was 'Criticism'.

It began in Germany but it rapidly spread to English and Scottish universities. The idea was that the Bible is nothing more than a human book, subject to all the errors of a human book, subject to all the mistaken ideas of imperfect, human thinking and that this book must be radically revised in the light of scientific and rational enquiry. Out must go the miracles, because science doesn't believe in the supernatural. Out must go the predictions of the prophets because you cannot predict the future. Out must go everything that is divine. Some incredible ideas came out of this school, such as the idea that Moses never wrote anything ascribed to him, that Isaiah probably didn't, that all the books are in the wrong order and that, in fact, the first five books of the Bible were written last and the prophets were written first. There began a spate of cutting the Bible to pieces, criticising this and criticising that, which crept right in to the church. The devil knew what he was doing. If he could shake people's faith in the Bible, he knew that he would have won a great battle, and he did.

At first the church fought hard. Bishop Colenso was excommunicated because he said Moses probably never lived and Joshua was certainly a myth. He was turned out of his bishopric for saying it. Professor Robertson Smith lost his chair of Hebrew in the University of Edinburgh for similar views. But the movement became very widespread and by 1900 the professors teaching young men for the ministry had accepted to a remarkable degree the critical school of the Bible, without realising that these critics were not, in fact, scientific, but were importing their own philosophical ideas as they looked at the material. That is an easy and dangerous thing to do. It is easy for me to make up my mind first what I believe and criticise what doesn't fit in with my idea, and that is what was happening.

Suffice it to say that when the twentieth century opened, the people in the pews were thinking, 'We'll get right through to our goal, the evangelisation of the world in our generation. We will see a Christian world in the next century.' As a Prime Minister of Christian England said: 'Up and up and up and on and on and on!' The idea of evolution was not just applied to the animals; it was now applied to man. 'We are getting better and better and better. We are on a moving escalator to Utopia!' That idea did not finally collapse until the year 1914, when all the primitive bestiality of man reared its ugly head and that idea that we were getting better and better and better, and that the new world was just around the corner, collapsed in ruins among the trenches of the First World War. But in 1900 it was still held.

Alas! The Christians had not realised how the devil had mobilised his forces and had them working, and they did not realise that church after church, chapel after chapel in this land would see declining congregations and would see empty buildings; how men would go away to the war and come back physically but not come back spiritually; how preacher after preacher would lose confidence in the Bible and have nothing worth preaching; how even views of Christ and the gospel would be diluted until there was nothing much left.

11

SOME TWENTIETH CENTURY DEVELOPMENTS

The early years of the twentieth century were marked by unbounded optimism and confidence in the Western world. The capitalists were still thoroughly secure in their wealth. Workers began to benefit from the struggles of trade unionism. The British Empire ruled the world, or so they thought, and the Navy kept that protected. The twentieth century was going to be Utopia, an unparalleled period of peace and prosperity for all.

Darwin's doctrine of evolution had now been applied to society and it was believed that evolution would sweep us upward into the brave new world.

Such optimism was very quickly shattered by two World Wars, the like of which the human race had never seen before, and the untold suffering and the cruelty and almost barbarian malice of those two great events shook that confidence.

The church itself shared that early optimism and there were many Christians who believed that within the twentieth century the church would spread through the whole globe and dominate the world, and certainly the figures were encouraging. In 1800, nominal Christians made up about 19% of the world's population. Entering the twentieth century, that had increased to 29.5%, and it looked as if the goal of spreading the church in the whole world was within reach.

But what was thought to be an easy century of progress, spiritual, physical, material, moral, became instead an era of terrible conflict. Here are some of the factors that entered into the world of the twentieth century which made the work of the church much more difficult, all of which are 'isms'.

Obviously the growing *secularism* of society was a new feature. Hitherto, Christians were battling with other religions. Now they were dealing with people who had no religion. People were living without any religion, never mind the Christian God. This growing secularism was one of the things that made this conflict of the twentieth century. The spread of *Communism* was another big factor. It spread over a third of the human race and by and large where Communism has spread, the door to missionary work seemed to close. There were hundreds of foreign missionaries in China when the twentieth century began, but they had been expelled by the 1960s, though when China opened up subsequently, it was clear that much had been happening clandestinely and Christianity had begun to explode on a massive scale.

Another factor was the rise of what we call *nationalism*, in which new nations were being born at a fantastic rate and were beginning to regard missionaries as foreigners. 'Western imperialists' was the tag that was sometimes hung round their necks, but the idea that a foreigner could come and teach us, this new nation, what religion we ought to have, was becoming increasingly repugnant.

There was the 'Disintegration of Western civilisation', (I am quoting here Professor Gilbert Murray) – the breakdown of Western society which had been the mainspring of the spread of missionary work, and the moral and spiritual breakdown in the West was a factor that the church had to cope with.

Yet another factor was the revival of ancient religions. Other religions had seemed to be dying out, but in the twentieth century they were growing again in some areas. Buddhism in Ceylon (now Sri Lanka) was one example of this. Islam in many places was another. There was a growth of cults, presenting a perverted kind of Christianity; in fact, not a Christianity at all when carefully examined. There were thousands of towns and villages in the world where no Christian missionary has been but who have had a Jehovah's Witness or Mormon visit.

These, and many other factors, meant that the twentieth century was a battleground for the church, and many thought that Christianity was going to have to fight for its life. Some even went so far as to predict that by the middle of the century the church would be well nigh finished. But let me anticipate that by saying that the church has never been bigger than it then became, never been more widespread geographically. There have never been more Christians in the world than there are now. That helps us to keep the thing in balance.

When you are living in a situation it is very difficult to see it objectively and to realise what is important and lasting and what is insignificant and transitory. Reviewing the twentieth century as it appeared back in the late 1960s, I identified three significant things that had happened *within* the church and we needed to be considering at that time. I believed that the significant things of history are what happen within the church. In the last analysis, I believe that God is writing the history of the world and that God's people are the key to it.

The three 'isms' which it was clear by the late 1960s were changing church life were: liberalism, ecumenism and Pentecostalism. At that time I summarised what was happening in those three directions and gave an assessment of them.

One of the big influences on Christianity in the twentieth century was undoubtedly liberalism. Though the seeds of this were sown in the nineteenth century, the flower came out in the twentieth. Like many other things, its source was Germany, which has produced some of the best-known thinkers, philosophers and theologians of the world. We do wrong if we underestimate the influence of Germany, particularly German thought, on the whole Western world.

By and large there is a pattern. What the German philosophers think today, the British philosophers will think tomorrow, the American philosophers will think the day after and the rest of the world will consider after that. There is a kind of pattern here which is a very significant move.

What was the heart of what we call liberalism? I can say it in a sentence from a penetrating assessment, entitled *'The Death and Resurrection of the Church* by Leslie Paul, an Anglican writer who was looking at the Church of England and trying to say what it needed to do in the twentieth century. He finished the book like this: 'No faith can live on the denial of its past and the rejection of its foundations.' The new and pace-making theology is often asking just that. The final crisis for the churches is this: 'What does Christianity assert as the ultimate and inevitable foundation of its faith?'

Paul went right to the heart of it. The crisis facing the church was this: 'What, in the last analysis, is the foundation for what you believe?' and it is the answer to that question which divided professing Christians into three camps: liberal, Catholic and evangelical. All three would speak of the church, the Bible and experience, but when church, Bible and experience seem to say contradictory things, the ultimate foundation is the one of those three which you choose to test the other two. The Catholic would say the church is the ultimate foundation and the church will interpret both the Bible and the experience. The evangelical says the Bible is the ultimate foundation and by it you must test the church and your experience. The liberal would say your experience is the final foundation and by your experience you must test the Bible and the church.

Now that is an over-simplification but basically that is what it means and the term 'liberal' means those who may use the Bible and may believe in the church but ultimately use their own *experience* to test truth, whether it is their mental experience, or their moral experience or their spiritual experience.

Now it is quite obvious that if experience decides what is true, there are certain things which the church has taught over the centuries about which you will become less sure. Heaven is one. I have had no experience whatever of the place called 'heaven'. How do I know it exists? The Bible says it does but how do I know? It is outside my *experience*. Even more important: hell is something which no one has ever yet experienced. Don't ever believe those who say you make your own hell on earth. You do nothing of the sort. Hell is something right outside my experience, and if I judge truth by experience I will not be very sure of it. Miracles are another case in point. The Bible is full of miracles, but there are many people today who have had no experience of miracles and therefore they question supernatural events. The wrath of God is something that none of us have experienced in its fullness, yet – none of us! One day, God is going to reveal his wrath against the sin of the world but he hasn't done so yet; not since the days of Noah has he done it and therefore it is outside our experience and therefore one can begin to question the wrath of God if experience is the test of truth.

I have given you enough to indicate the kind of direction that this moves in. Question the miracles, question heaven, and above all, hell, question the wrath of God, and above all, question the sin of man because surely my experience is that people are very nice! Oh they have their faults, but my experience, surely, is not that they are sinners, destined for hell – those nice people living next door to me? If experience is the test I could find it very difficult to believe that.

The American theologian H. Richard Niebuhr (brother of Reinhold) critiqued the social gospel, writing of a 'God without wrath', who, 'brought men without sin into a kingdom without judgment through the ministrations of a Christ without a cross.' (See *The Kingdom of God in America*, Chicago, 1937). That is a very good summary and that was the kind of devastating idea that came into the church. What then is left of the gospel? What is the good news? If you cut hell out, if you cut sin out, if you cut God's wrath out, what is the gospel?

The answer is that you would have to find another kind of gospel, and find it they did. On the one hand were those who found what they called the *social* gospel, a new 'gospel' in which supposedly the good news was 'Christianise the social order'. There were others who had a *psychological* gospel, who said that Jesus saves you from your neuroses. Jesus saves you from your guilt complex, rather than your sins. Jesus saves you from your frustrations and repressions, and conversion is simply a psychological integration.

So whether it was the social gospel or the psychological, the belief basically was that man was not as bad as the old-fashioned preachers made out and hell was not man's destination.

It seemed by the 1960s that the two World Wars had dented that kind of liberalism. War had shown two young Swiss thinkers, Karl Barth and Emil Brunner, that man was not getting better and better, that sin was a reality, and that that wrath of God over it was real, and that war is an example of the kind of consequence that fallen human nature produces. Barth and Brunner became famous names in twentieth century theology, and you will find their books on every minister's shelves. They swung the pendulum back, and they began again to preach sin, to preach atonement by the cross, to preach the wrath of God and the mercy of God, and it looked for a time as if the gospel was going to be preached again as once it was preached by our forefathers. Alas, that did not happen. Why? Because though they swung back in so many things, to sin, to atonement, to everything else, there was one thing they didn't swing back to and it was the crucial thing: they didn't swing back to believing that the Bible was the word of God. They remained with the liberal idea that the Bible was a book of human experience exactly the same as any other book and must be treated that way. It must be examined in exactly the same way as you would examine the Domesday Book and the Magna Carta.

This was the difficulty: they tried to swing back to a biblical gospel without going back to the view of the Bible as the word of God and the result demonstrated that you can't hold people there without the Bible. You can't preach what is in the Bible unless you believe it to be true. You can't convince people of the truth of Bible teaching unless you yourself are convinced that it is a true book. So the pendulum began to swing back again to the new form of liberalism which doesn't go by that name. It began to be termed 'Radicalism', but it is the same old thing in a new dress, promulgated by writers like Bultmann and Tillich – both of them Germans incidentally. Once again, they started a fashion in philosophy and theology until through the popularisers in this country, like the Bishop of Woolwich and others in America, it swung so far back that theologians, training men for the ministry, announced 'God is dead'. What did they mean by that? They didn't mean they had stopped believing in God. They meant that the God of the old-fashioned preacher was dead. We had a poster ready to display at Easter, saying: 'Our God is not dead. Sorry about yours!' Those who said 'God is dead' meant that the God my grandfather believed in was dead, the God who is angry with sinners and sends them to hell is dead. It was another twentieth century idea.

A professor of Church History in Yale University was asked at that time to comment on the chaos of belief in the Protestant churches, and he said this: 'None of us is sure what we believe but let us unbelieve together.' I ask you! If that is the only unity we could have, it would not make much impact on the world outside. Unity must be based on truth. We must agree on what we believe, then we will make an impact.

Two groups resisted liberalism very strongly. On the one hand the Roman Catholics resisted it because they felt that experience was not the test but the church was. And in 1950 the Pope promulgated a new belief that the assumption of the Virgin Mary's body after her death, the ascension of her body to heaven, was now part of the Christian faith. It was in this way that he asserted that for Rome at least, the church is the final arbiter of truth.

The other group that resisted this movement, and thank God, the majority of Protestants are in this group, though not in this country, were the evangelicals who said: 'For us, the Bible is the arbiter of truth about Christ, not the church, not my experience, both of which must be examined by the word of God which we believe is contained in holy scripture'. I suppose the evangelicals found at least one spokesman in the most famous preacher of the twentieth century, a Baptist called Billy Graham, whose catchword 'The Bible says....!' became a very real and popular expression of the evangelical position.

Liberalism was the first 'ism'. The second to become a big factor by the 1960s was ecumenism. Archbishop Temple said, 'This was the great new fact of our era.' I have spoken about an 'ism' which is wholly bad. I now speak about an 'ism' which is very complex because it is so mixed, and I want to try to be absolutely fair. Let us first get the word 'ecumenical' clear. It is a word many use but very few understand. It comes from a Greek word *oikumene*, signifying 'the whole inhabited world' (deriving from *oikein*, to inhabit) and this word has been taken up to mean a movement for the unity of Christians in the whole inhabited world, the ecumenical sphere.

Let us look at how it developed. Key dates to remember are 1910, 1948 and 1961. First of all let me tell you about the movement for unity before 1910. Every book I have read on the ecumenical movement says it began in 1910. That is not true, it began years earlier. It really began in the nineteenth century. It could have been said to have begun when William Carey suggested that Christians from all over the world met at the Cape of Good Hope for fellowship. That was the first suggestion of a meeting for unity, and it was at the end of the eighteenth century that that was said. But it was in the nineteenth century that Christians felt the need for unity. But note that it was the evangelicals who felt the need for this unity and who first began to establish it.

The Evangelical Alliance was formed in 1845

and began to jump the gulf between denominations. Movements like the Student Christian Movement (SCM) and Young Men's Christian Association (YMCA)which in their early days were thoroughly evangelical, aimed at creating unity between Christians of different denominations. In 1875, Keswick meetings began under a banner 'All One in Christ Jesus' and brought Christians of all denominations together. At the beginning of the twentieth century there were such movements as The Federal Council of Evangelical Churches in Britain. Later the word 'evangelical' was dropped out and 'Free' was put in and it became 'The Free Church Federal Council'.

At the same time, the denominations of the world were beginning to form world denominational fellowships including the Baptist World Alliance and the Methodist World Council. These came into being in the first ten years of last century so that you had evangelical unity across the denominations and international denominational fellowships forming. That was the pattern until 1910.

In 1910, the missionaries of the world came together in Edinburgh because they had a burden, which I can put simply. A friend of mine went to India, met an Indian Christian and said, 'I am so glad to meet an Indian Christian.' And the Indian Christian replied, 'But I'm a Canadian Baptist'! That kind of silly thing caused the 'burden'. We have taken our ideas, our organisations, our labels all over the world, and instead of leading people to

Christ we have made them this, that or the other. In the 1960s that mistake was generally not being made so much in Latin America but it was made by missionary societies all over the world in the nineteenth century, and there was the realisation that we had locked Christians up in their own little compartments, separated from others with different labels. So it was that missionaries came together in 1910 and said, 'This is ridiculous. What is the answer?'

The tragedy is that there are two possible answers and they didn't discuss both! One answer is to do away with denomination labels and indeed, to do away with denominations. The other answer is to unite the denominations in one big denomination and label it one. They only considered the second and out of that Conference came a number of things. As far as Latin America was concerned, it stimulated evangelicals to unite and as the Evangelical Union of South America.

But from Edinburgh came various movements, one to examine beliefs, called 'Faith and Order', and one to examine behaviour, called 'Life and Work', and these two movements gradually coalesced until, in 1938, the World Council of Churches (WCC) was formed. The War prevented it from ever acting as such and it was not until ten years later, in 1948, that the WCC was actually able to meet in its own name, in Amsterdam.

During the period 1910 – 1948 numerous unions had taken place. In Canada (1925), Methodists,

Congregationals and Presbyterians became the United Church of Canada. In South India (1947), Methodists, Congregationals, Presbyterians and Anglicans became the Church of South India. In 1929 three different groups in Scotland became the Church of Scotland. In 1932 three different groups of Methodists became The Methodist Church.

In the World Council of Churches, 147 denominations from 44 countries declared an intention to stay together. Now that sounds a very impressive number but the majority of Christians remained *outside* the World Council of Churches. We heard a lot about the WCC in the 1960s and the subsequent decades, and many presumed that it was the only union of Christians. It is not, it is only one among others. Eastern Orthodox churches joined, but it has never included the Roman Catholics, who maintain a discreet distance but are friendly towards it. It has never included the vast majority of Baptists or of evangelicals generally but it has included the Episcopal (Anglican), Methodist, Presbyterian and Congregational streams.

In 1961, at the WCC meeting in New Delhi, the shift in emphasis was from Unity to Union. There was now a plea to the churches, not just to have unity with one another but to go all out for union, and unity locally was defined in terms of organised union.

In the mid-1960s, the Nottingham Faith and Order Conference in Britain took this up and with a ringing and imaginative plea, asked the churches in Britain to arrange for organic union of the denominations in England by Easter Day 1980, and that date caught the imagination of many denominations. Anglicans and Methodists were engaged in negotiations as were Presbyterians and Congregationals. Why did the Romans stay out? Precisely because they believe the *church* is, in the last analysis, the arbiter of truth. Why did evangelicals stay out? For the most part because they believe the *Bible* is the final arbiter of truth.

Since 1910 the ecumenical movement has largely been a partner of the liberal thinking. There have been many wonderful Christians in it, men of the calibre and stature of John R. Mott, J. H. Oldham, Bishop Bell and many others that I have mentioned. Evangelicals, in staying out, are not saying that those who are in are not Christians, they are saying we do not believe the church of Christ is made up of all the denominations, we believe it is made up of all those who are born again of the Holy Spirit. We do not believe that unity is to be a thing of visible organisation. We believe that Christ, the night before he died, prayed that his disciples would be one, as he and his Father were one, which was not a visible unity, but a unity of heart, mind and wills.

Evangelicals feel that until there is a unity of heart and mind and will, organisational unity is a mockery of the real thing. It is for these and many other reasons that the majority of evangelicals in the world have stayed outside. Nevertheless, many evangelicals desire to talk and to have fellowship with those sincere Christians who belong to the Lord and who are struggling within the movement to see that it produces the real thing.

The biggest question over it which, to my mind, needs to be answered, is what was the primary inspiration of this? Is it Satanic, is it human or is it divine? That may sound an incredibly blasphemous question to you, but I believe a very good case can be made out for all three possibilities and it is because it is such a mixture of all three, that one has, not a red light, not a green light but a yellow light saying: Caution; go steadily. As Gamaliel said, 'If this is of God' it will last. If it is not, it will come to nothing.

I do not believe the church of Jesus Christ will ever be visibly one this side of heaven. I think if you got everybody into one organisation tomorrow morning, someone would have broken away from it by next Sunday and started another fellowship, but the real unity is the unity of the Holy Spirit which is to be found in all Christians of all denominations who have been born again of the Spirit, who know and love the Lord Jesus. You will find some of those if you move from church to church, but wherever you find them you will find that within minutes you can have fellowship with them. That is the basic unity.

The one good thing, to my mind, that this movement did was to stimulate evangelicals to closer unity both in the World Evangelical Fellowship and in local, national evangelical groups. There has been a coming together of those who love the Lord and his word in this country and overseas that is going to be more and more powerful in the future.

Now the third 'ism' I come to is Pentecostalism. It was born around the beginning of the twentieth century. Funnily enough, for getting a First in some exams, I was presented with a church history volume, a great thick thing, by the great Baptist scholar in America, Kenneth Scott Latourette, and it is a wonderful history of two thousand years of the church. I am indebted to it. It is a wonderful compendium of fact and if you want to read about 1,500 pages, that is the book to get. But I looked in vain for any mention of the fastest growing, and now the largest Protestant group in the world, the Pentecostals. Not a mention, and it goes right up to 1950. I find that an incredible blind spot. I know it is the youngest of all the groups but by the 1960s it could be said that it was the fastest growing movement, without any shadow of a doubt, particularly in Latin America, but also in North America, Africa and parts of Asia.

This movement, like Christianity itself, was born in a stable; in Azusa Street, in Los Angeles, in the year 1906. It came because some people were praying hard for a revival of the Spirit of God, feeling that as they came into the twentieth century, unless the Holy Spirit did something new, things would go terribly wrong. Things began to happen there which at first they did not understand themselves but which later they were able to understand.

There was a Methodist minister in Oslo, Norway, the Rev. T. B. Barratt, who went to New York enquiring about this. He had been helped by the Welsh Revival of 1904 but he realised there was something more here. He went to New York. He never reached Los Angeles except by correspondence from New York, but he returned to Norway with a remarkable experience of the Holy Spirit. The Rev. Alexander Boddie of All Saints' Anglican church, Sunderland, heard of Barratt and asked him to come to All Saints, and a revival broke out in Sunderland in the year 1907. From that small beginning in Los Angeles, in Oslo, in Sunderland, County Durham, what is now the largest Protestant group has emerged, numbering by the 1960s some 30 million members and many more adherents. In fact, Baptists and Pentecostals have become the two largest Protestant groups.

In Latin America, the Pentecostal growth was absolutely astonishing. A Methodist minister who was a missionary in Latin America with a group of American Methodists was asked to leave that group because of his Pentecostal leanings. It then numbered 4000 members. Ten years later he had seen a revival which had 25,000 members and the Methodist Mission he had left still had its 4000. (In the forty years or so since the late 1960s, even more dramatic growth has been seen.)

This made people ask questions, particularly in

1960, when what was (wrongly) called 'New Pentecostalism' appeared within mainline denominations, beginning with the Episcopalians of America but spreading rapidly through others.

Without giving you the history, may I go straight to the doctrine. What is the heart of the movement we call Pentecostalism which covers the first six decades of the twentieth century? After a lot of reading and a bit of experience, and much fellowship and discussion with Pentecostals, I came to the conclusion that whatever they would say is at the heart of it, it is *a real belief in supernatural experience*. This is expressed in two fundamental teachings and the onus is on all those who are not Pentecostal to examine the scriptures as the disciples at Berea did and 'see whether these things be so'.

The first is that there is a Baptism in the Holy Spirit which is a conscious experience for all Christians to seek, and which is neither automatic nor unconscious at the time of conversion, an experience which may take place at the time of conversion and may not; and, if not, will need to be sought later; and, secondly, that a Baptism in the Spirit will make possible the exercise of supernatural abilities, called in the scriptures 'gifts of the Spirit', gifts of healing, gifts of praising God in unknown languages, gifts of interpreting those languages, gifts of miracle working, gifts of extraordinary knowledge, gifts of supernatural wisdom, gifts of special faith and so on.

Now until the Pentecostals said this, it was widely believed in the other churches that these things, which you read about in the Bible, ceased with the apostles, and that the power of the Holy Spirit as it was made manifest in Acts was a kind of booster stage of a rocket, and once the rocket was in orbit the booster stage fell off. Once the church was going, these things were no longer needed. That was the general view.

But in the late 1960s we needed to go back and say, 'Is there anything in the scripture that says that these things are not for us today?' I searched the scriptures and could find nothing that says the gifts are not for today – which means that, as the Pentecostals were saying, 1 Corinthians 12–14 needed to be taken very seriously indeed by the church, and that such things were still possible, so Pentecost was not just an anniversary in the church calendar but an experience for every believer who seeks for such power.

There are dangers with all power, of course, and the abuses, excesses, division, emotionalism and fanaticism that sometimes arose are well known – indeed, if you look in the letters of Paul to the Corinthians you will find that the gifts were accompanied by those very abuses there. But what Paul does *not* say is 'Scrap the gifts because of the abuses!' just as he did not say 'Scrap the communion!' because they were getting drunk at Holy Communion. The answer to people getting drunk at Communion is not to stop Communion but to stop them getting drunk, and Paul would have said that the answer to abuse of spiritual gifts is not to stop them but to use them rightly and properly, and there is a right way to use them.

One of the greatest lacks of the Pentecostal movement has been sound biblical teaching that would keep everything decent and in order, and would keep it where God wanted it to be. There are four safeguards needed against abuse and excess: the *word of God* tells you how to use the gifts for the good of others; the *reason* of man, not such an emphasis on the emotion that the reason departs; the *discipline* of the church; and the *holiness* of the believer. Given those four things, I realised that they could add a great deal to the church, but quite frankly, when this began to happen, most of the older churches were like old bottles having new wine poured in.

Let me summarise this by mentioning some things I learned from the Pentecostal movement which I believe every church has to learn. It is a movement of the *common people*. I mean no disrespect at all here, but I am speaking very plainly. Abraham Lincoln said, 'The Lord must love common people. He has made so many of them.' What I mean is this: churches that depend on natural gifts become thoroughly bourgeois and middle class but Pentecostalism has shown us that supernatural gifts have no regard to persons and that anybody who loves the Lord and is filled with the Spirit can lead the church. Therefore, to put it in blunt terms, I think there is something in the criticism that was made in this rather crude phrase: 'The ecclesiastical bourgeoisie and the Pentecostal proletariat'. But it is the one movement in the twentieth century that broke out of the middle class straitjacket of the church, and I rejoice in that and think we can learn from it. When God gives spiritual gifts he doesn't look at the degrees after a person's name, he doesn't look at their educational diplomas, he doesn't look at the size of their house, he distributes his gifts as he wills.

The second thing I learned is that if people have their tongues loosened in praise, *they will have their tongues loosened for witness*, and one of the reasons why Christians don't speak about Christ outside the church more is that they don't speak to Christ inside the church more, and I am sure that worship benefits when the Spirit prompts anyone to lead in worship and enables anyone to do so. Congregational worship I have already mentioned.

This is the biggest thing I have learned: *faith to expect to see God work*. The ultimate answer to the 'God is dead' movement is to see the work of the Holy Spirit. That is an unanswerable answer. A move of the Holy Spirit answers the 'God is dead' movement and declares that this God, this 'old-fashioned' God in whom we believe is still alive and is still able to save and to change lives and is still able to perform miracles.

It is to believe in a *living* God, a *miraculous* and *supernatural* God. That is what I learned.

We have seen that the twentieth century was very difficult for the church, but not impossible. With God all things are possible. Some doors closed but others were opening wide. Latin America opened as we noted. Later, other formerly 'closed' regions were opened up too.

It may not have been seen in Britain, but around the world the church was growing, even back in the late 1960s. On the encouraging side, the Bible was still the best seller. The Wycliffe Bible translators who started in 1933 tackled hundreds of languages. There are over 3,600 languages in the world and there were some 1,600 done by 1933 and the Wycliffe Bible translators under the title '2000 tongues to go' said, 'We are going to tackle the rest and make sure that everybody can read the word of God in their own language'.

I noted in the 1960s that radio and television in the UK were not as available to Christians as in some other countries, but that has since changed dramatically with the advent of commercial satellite and cable broadcasting and the internet.

Above all, there was growing missionary zeal in the course of the twentieth century, which is continuing in the twenty-first. We have come to think that America is at the forefront of this now, and in a sense this is true. Britain is no longer the leader of the world in sending out missionaries and money, America is. But one of the most exciting facts of the twentieth century was that the younger churches of Africa, Asia and Latin America became missionary-minded churches, sending out their own missionaries. It changed the whole pattern of the China Inland Mission which moved its headquarters from Britain to Singapore so that it might send nationals from their churches to other nations. It was no longer just West to East and North to South. The time came when believers started to come from these places to our country to tell the pagans of Britain who have never heard about the Lord Jesus Christ.

12

THE CHURCH IN THE FUTURE

Back in the late 1960s I met many pessimistic Christians who thought that the church was on the way out and that Christianity would die out. But, as we know, that hasn't happened. One of the most encouraging facts to me is a continuing growth in the worldwide spread in availability of the scriptures in so many languages, and the hunger for God's word in the Bible. People still want good news because there is so much bad news and this book contains the good news.

When the early church ran into its first difficulties and some of the Christians were put in prison, one of the wise men on the bench in the courtroom that heard their case said this: 'In the present case, I tell you, keep away from these men and let them alone for if this plan, or this undertaking is of men it will fail, but if it is of God you will not be able to overthrow them. You might even be found opposing God.'

Those were the words of Gamaliel, and they

are worth recalling as we look forward. I suppose in the year 1900 people thought that one day the church would come right in, that one day the church would cover the whole world and everybody would become Christians and the whole world would be a Christian world. That was the Christian belief, to a very large degree, about 1900. It was swept in on the wave of optimism of the spreading British Empire and all the rest, and if you read the average missionary hymn which comes from that era, you will find that very optimistic view clearly there in those hymns. But I want to say very clearly I do not believe that will ever come. My hope is not centred on the church converting everybody in the world and, in fact, we are fighting a losing battle with the population explosion now and there are not many Christians who are thinking that way these days.

Now if 1900 said the church will come right in, 1950 found a lot of people saying the church is going right out – and taking the opposite view, the pessimistic view, which believes that the church is a dying cause and finished. I would agree that if you go into many churches you might well feel that, but it would be a mistaken conclusion.

We turn now to the last few decades, then the future which I cannot date but in which certain events will take place within time, and then the ultimate future of the church in eternity – beyond the dating of history.

I could spend a lot of time speculating concerning the church's beliefs or the church's behaviour.

Here are some of my speculations. I believe that the church will never be visibly united in one organisation, in history. I don't expect that. I don't believe it could happen.

Secondly, I believe the church will become less institutional and less clerical. I think the future Christianity will be the informal Christianity that may not have buildings and may not have clergymen with their collars back to front but may spring up everywhere spontaneously within homes, within places of work, in all sorts of other ways.

I believe that the leadership of the church is going to pass from the northern hemisphere to the southern hemisphere and that the churches that have been traditionally the 'senders' of the gospel and the 'givers' of Christianity will need to become the 'receivers', and this will humble them greatly.

As far as beliefs are concerned, we look at the three-fold division I have made between Catholic, liberal and evangelical (or whatever other labels are used; for example: evangelicals are sometimes called fundamentalists and liberals are sometimes called neo-orthodox) – but whatever the labels, there are three groups. In the late 1960s I predicted that all those in the middle group, or the main denominations affected, namely Anglican, Presbyterian, Methodist and Congregational, were likely to draw much closer together, and indeed were likely to unite in many countries, as they did in Canada and South India and were seeking to do in Pakistan – and in England, for the Anglicans and the Methodists were talking together, as were Congregationals and Presbyterians, and have since become the United Reformed Church.

I also hazarded a speculation that that would not make much difference to their impact on the world. In the last analysis, it is truth that makes the impact, not unity, and people do not stay away from churches because they are not united, but because they are bewildered, not getting a clear voice ('This is what we believe.')

Now of those who do give the clear voice, frankly, the field will be left to the Catholics and the evangelicals – those who say, 'This is what the church says', and those who say, 'This is what the Bible says'.

I think the Catholics if they go on adapting themselves in method (as they are doing) are likely to gain ground. They are losing it in Southern Europe but they may gain ground in Northern Europe and elsewhere in the world.

Evangelicals will become at once more united and more divided, for various reasons. I think this trend will become more pronounced over the next few decades.

Now all this is speculation and it makes this one big assumption: that present trends are going to continue in the same direction. But the one fact I have left out is the fact of the possibility of God the Holy Spirit breaking in on the situation, and that could completely change all that I have said because I set no limits to what the Holy Spirit can do in any church, in any denomination, in any country and in any person, and present trends can be completely reversed. They have been in England from time to time, when the Holy Spirit has poured out revival on our country and history has been changed. Pray God that we might live to see again such a revival as this country has seen, but mark my words, it will not come as it came before. No revival ever repeats another and you need to be watching carefully to see where God is working, sometimes in the most unexpected places and through the most unexpected people.

But having said all that, which is speculation and has made no allowance for what the Holy Spirit might do, may I tell you of some things of which I am certain because God has said so in the scriptures.

Firstly, the gospel will go to every nation in the world. There are Christians on every continent but there are still some areas in the world where the gospel has not been heard until recently. I believe that God has willed that the gospel should go to every nation, every tribe, every people, every tongue, and if God has willed that, it will be done and the church is doing it in his will. That is not to say that everybody will be converted but that everybody will hear, and with modern methods of mass communication I believe it is within our reach.

Second, he has also told us very clearly that there will be a great falling away and that the love of many Christians will grow cold – in other words, a world full of backsliding Christians. I find that an ominous and a terrible thought but it is there and I cannot avoid it in the Bible. Britain is full of backsliding Christians! You go out and stop the first man in the street and say, 'Did you go to Sunday school? Did you hear about Jesus when you were a child?' You will be amazed how many people there are whose love has grown cold and how many set off well as young people.

Why? For many reasons: false teaching coming in, perverted ideas of Christianity, preachers who play to the gallery and preach fancies and fables simply because people want to hear something new instead of something old.

But the biggest reason for this will be my third prediction from the Scripture: that persecution of Christians will increase and increase. It will be more and more difficult to stand for Jesus Christ and the church of Jesus Christ will need to prepare now for difficult days ahead. It is going to be increasingly difficult to live the Christian life as history draws to its final, catastrophic denouement.

So much for the immediate future. May I now pass on to the *intermediate* future of the church. What is the next great world event? It is mentioned three hundred times in the New Testament – not the cross, that is past, though it is mentioned three hundred times, but the return of our Lord Jesus Christ to this world in physical, visible form, coming back in a body that has nail prints in hands and feet. When this happens, the condition of the church will be radically changed.

All Christians who love the word of God believe that Jesus Christ is coming again and believe the same thing about the day when he comes, but Christians are divided (or, at least, differ) over what is to happen before he comes and what is to happen afterwards, and it is about these two things that I want to write briefly, and all I can do is to share with you purely on the grounds of my own understanding. After my years of studying the New Testament I can only tell you what I find therein and leave you to study it for yourself and see what you can find in those pages.

The three events which concern us here are given technical names by many Christians: the tribulation, the rapture and the millennium. We are agreed about the middle one. There is some difference of understanding about the tribulation. There is some difference of understanding about the millennium. But let me tell you what these three words mean and emphasise that middle one and underline it. Get your hope fixed there.

First of all, the *tribulation* is a term we use, sometimes – 'the great tribulation' which is a biblical phrase, for the final few years of history when there will be terrible trouble. The word 'tribulation' means 'trouble', from the Latin *tribulum* which was used of a threshing sledge, with spikes underneath that ran over the corn to separate it from the chaff, and the tribulation is when you feel everything is going over you and ripping you to bits. So the great tribulation is a few years at the end of history when history goes wrong. They will be years of tyranny when there will be a world dictator and a world religion, a totalitarian state which in return for peace and security makes a total claim on the human race, not just physically but mentally and spiritually, and does that by establishing dictator worship.

Now we have seen the horrors of totalitarian states. Some of us have lived through such horrors, and every totalitarian state, sooner or later, plunges its people into war and suffering. That, multiplied on a world scale, is what is meant by the great tribulation in scripture. A climax of totalitarian government at the end of history that will plunge people ultimately into a major war.

Christians differ over what will happen to the church during the great tribulation at the end of history. Many sincere Christians for whom I have a profound respect but from whom I must in love differ, believe that the church will be taken out of the world before that tribulation. It is an idea that never appeared until the nineteenth century, and then it appeared in two people: Edward Irving a Presbyterian and J.N. Darby an Anglican curate. From J.N. Darby it passed to all the groups known as the Brethren, and through what is called the Scofield Bible the idea has passed to many other Christians. I can only say that I have been unable to find this in the scripture. I can find it in the Scofield

Bible; I can find it in books by many people, but I have yet to meet a person who found it by reading the Bible alone.

Others believe that the church will be taken out of the tribulation half way through and others, and here I frankly put myself, believe that the church will go through that trouble and that Jesus will come at the end of it and take them out. This is my own understanding of scripture. At least the only way out of that trouble, as I can see it, will be by martyrdom.

Now why is it that that will be a time of such trouble for God's people? The answer is very simple. There are two groups of people who never fit in to a totalitarian state: Jews and Christians. They are the only two groups of people in totalitarian states in the past who have said, 'We cannot worship man' – even for the price of peace and security. It is God's people who will suffer most and I believe personally that the church must be prepared for that and must be ready to go through that trouble as she has come through other troubles and looked for the appearing of Jesus Christ who will come to rescue his church and come to take them to be with himself.

Now if you do not hold the view that I have come to, then God bless you and let us agree to differ in love. May I plead with you not to read any Bibles with notes in but go to the word of God with an open mind and say, 'What does scripture say?'

But the second thing of the intermediate future

I can be more dogmatic on: the rapture. What will happen when Jesus comes back? I tell you this, if you have never flown before, you will fly then. It is, as I have said, the noisiest verse in the Bible. The trumpet will sound, the archangel will cry and with a shout the Lord will descend from heaven. It will be a shout loud enough to wake the dead and the first people to meet him on that day will be those who have died, and the second group of people to meet him on that day will be those who are still living. That means one generation of Christians will never die. There will be no more funerals for one group of Christians. That is an exciting, thrilling thing to me. Yet it is a sobering thought too.

I remember the final rally of a Billy Graham crusade at Wembley, and looking round at what may have been over a hundred thousand Christians and others singing the praises of God in the stands and I remember thinking: this is a big meeting but what kind of a meeting will it be up there in the clouds with Jesus? Every Christian who has ever lived! There won't be a stadium big enough on earth, so Jesus has arranged to meet us in the air. That is big enough and you can imagine the crowd that there will be from every nation, from the dead, people of bygone years in one meeting. The biggest Christian meeting ever held. Furthermore, it will be the longest and they shall be forever with the Lord. But the Bible reminds us of this, that those who meet Christ in the air – and what an exhilarating experience that will be, even physically – those who are taken to meet him will leave others behind. In one of the most sobering things he ever uttered, Jesus said, *'There will be two women in one kitchen and one will go and the other will be left. There will be two people in the same bed and husband or wife will be left alone in a double bed.'* It will be an extraordinary day when Jesus calls the church home. May I solemnly ask you if you are quite sure that you will be meeting in that great Christian rally at the end of history? You need to be sure. Even if your spouse is sure, that doesn't mean that you will be there. You may drag your unbelieving husband or wife to a church service but you won't be able to drag them to that meeting. *'One will be taken'*, said Jesus, *'and the other will be left'* but what a sight and a sound it will be when we meet the Lord Jesus. That is why my grandfather has on his gravestone: 'What a meeting!' – a comment which puzzles those who enjoy looking round at tombstones.

The third thing that I mentioned concerning the intermediate future was the millennium, a Latin word meaning a thousand years. (A word that has been used is 'Chilianism', from the Greek: *chilian*.) The New Testament speaks of a thousand years at the end of history, after Christ comes again, in which he will reign in this world. Christians do differ in their understanding of this. Some believe that this is a purely symbolic figure and does not mean a period of time. Others believe that the church is to start that thousand years and Christ will come at the end of it, and others, including myself, feel that it means what it says and that there will be a thousand years in which Christ will show what he can do when he is in charge of this world. This is a world that was meant to be God's world. The devil got hold of it and the devil runs it at the moment. *'We know we are of God and the whole world lieth in the power of the evil one.'* Jesus called the devil *'the god of this world'*. He is running it. If you want to know why there are wars being fought it is because Satan is running the world, and if you solve one conflict tomorrow there will be another war somewhere else the next week because he is running it. Why is it that we can't, with all our resources, with all our knowledge, with all our science and education, create a world in which we are happy for our children to grow up? Because Satan is running it, that is why.

But what a wonderful world it could be if Jesus ran it. We would have peace because we would have justice. We would have the things that we were meant to have. We would have a world in which even the animals wouldn't prey on each other, and I believe that Jesus will show what he can do at the end of history when he takes over the government. I believe the government will be upon his shoulder one day and so I look forward to that in the intermediate future. But I am not going to say any more about it except to state that when I say, *'Thy kingdom come on earth as it is in heaven'* I mean just this, because that phrase *'on earth as it is in heaven'* applies to the three previous phrases. *'Hallowed be Thy name on earth as it is in heaven. Thy kingdom come on earth as it is in heaven. Thy will be done on earth as it is in heaven'.* It qualifies all three and I believe there will be a kingdom of Christ, that the kingdoms of this world must become the kingdoms of Christ and then he can hand them back to the Father and God will be all in all.

That brings me to the ultimate future that lies beyond, the third great stage in the future of the church. Surprisingly little is said about the ultimate future of the church because it is unimaginable!

May I say that the only thing I need to say here is this: *'What eye has not seen, what ear has not heard, what has never entered into the heart of man to conceive or imagine, God has prepared for them that love him'.*

So I can't tell you much about the ultimate future. I can tell you that it is as different as being engaged to being married. Wonderful to be engaged, to be in love, but to be married is the real thing and Paul said, *I have betrothed you, engaged you to Christ,* but one day there is going to be a marriage and the relationship to Christ in heaven will be as different from my relationship to Christ now as my relationship to my wife now is to when we were engaged, and that is something to look forward to.

You are going to be worshipping in heaven. It makes me ashamed when people grumble at the length of a service. When I think of Baptists in the old USSR who met in Moscow for three hours, and of the churches in Germany after the war, with their roofs off, no heating and ten degrees of frost, meeting for four and five hours, when I think of people in Latin America who don't want to go home from the service and just want to go on and on, why in Britain do we say, 'He's been an hour'?

Let me tell you first that God asked you to give him one day in seven, not a couple of hours in it. One day – and when you get to heaven you are going to be worshipping him all the time. When you really love the Lord, to worship him forever is heaven. It really is, and every time you have a foretaste of heaven down below you could go on worshipping, couldn't you?

You will be worshipping and serving him, day and night. 24-hour shifts! Never grumble that you are doing too much for the Lord, that he is loading you too much. You are going to be serving him day and night up there. What a wonderful preparation, to be doing as much as you can for the Lord here, serving him day and night.

I don't know what service there will be to render. I haven't been given the details. I just know that I won't be sitting all day in an armchair embroidered with the letters 'RIP'. I will be doing something. I will be serving God, busy doing the Lord's work day and night in his holy temple. It will be a most active place. In fact, so wonderful that I just can't describe it and neither could you even if you had been there.

Paul speaks of being '...caught up to the seventh heaven'. An unimaginable future for the church! The church does not look to the immediate future or even the intermediate. It looks right beyond and says there is an ultimate future in which there will be a new world – a new heaven and a new earth – and everybody in it will be in the church of Christ, and for the first time what I have always believed in but never seen, there will be one holy, catholic (which means universal), and apostolic church, for the apostles will be there in the centre of it. The glory of it all!

I believe that the only human society on earth that has a future is the church, mainly because it is the only society on earth that never loses a single member by death and the only society on earth that is bigger every minute of every hour of every day of every week of every month of every year of every decade of every century of every millennium and has been growing ever since Christ said, *'Peter I will build my church'*.

I have tried to trace the building of that church. How many times, when it seemed as if the church would die out, the Holy Spirit has brought the word of God and the gospel to people and it has sprung to life again and gone on growing.

There are three Christian virtues: faith, which builds on the past and what God has already done; hope, which builds on the future and what God is going to do; and love, which builds on the present. A Christian life is unbalanced that is strong in faith and even in love, but lacking in hope, and through this book I have been seeking to stimulate your hope, and for the Christian the word 'hope' does not mean, as it means to many other people 'wishful thinking'. It means absolute certainty for the future.

I finish with some words of the great man, Bishop Ryle, that great Anglican bishop of Liverpool of a former time. He has the little pamphlet called *The True Church* and he finishes: *Men fancy if they join this church or that church and become communicants or go through certain forms that all must be right with their souls. It is an utter delusion. It is a gross mistake. Take notice, you may be a staunch Anglican or Presbyterian or Congregational or Baptist or Methodist or Plymouth Brother and yet not belong to the true church and if you do not, it would be better, at last, if you had never been born.*

Books by David Pawson available from
www.davidpawson.org
www.davidpawson.com

Come with me through Galatians
Come with me through Isaiah
Come with me through Jude
Come with me through Mark
Come with me through Revelation
Christianity Explained
Defending Christian Zionism
The God and the Gospel of Righteousness
Is John 3:16 the Gospel?
Israel in the New Testament
Jesus Baptises in One Holy Spirit
Jesus: The Seven Wonders of HIStory
Leadership is Male
Living in Hope
Not As Bad As The Truth (autobiography)
Once Saved, Always Saved?
Practising the Principles of Prayer
Remarriage is Adultery Unless....
The Challenge of Islam to Christians
The Normal Christian Birth
The Road to Hell
When Jesus Returns
Where has the Body been for 2000 years?
Where is Jesus Now?
Why Does God Allow Natural Disasters?
Word and Spirit Together
Unlocking the Bible

Books by David Pawson are available in the USA from
www.pawsonbooks.com

Unlocking the Bible
is also available in DVD format from
www.davidpawson.com
Video on demand: www.christfaithmedia.com

EBOOKS

Most books by David Pawson are also available
as ebooks from:

amazon.com and amazon.co.uk Kindle stores.

**For details of foreign language editions
and a full listing of
David Pawson Teaching Catalogue in MP3/DVD
or to purchase David Pawson books in the UK**
please visit:
www.davidpawson.com

Email: info@davidpawsonministry.com

Chinese language books by David Pawson
www.bolbookstore.com
and
www.elimbookstore.com.tw

Made in the USA
Columbia, SC
16 June 2023

18177366R00150